W9-AVM-198

The Essential Vince Lombardi

The Essential Vince Lombardi

Words and Wisdom to Motivate, Inspire, and Win

Compiled, Introduced, and Annotated by

Vince Lombardi, Jr.

MCGRAW-HILL

New York   Chicago   San Francisco   Lisbon
London   Madrid   Mexico City   Milan   New Delhi
San Juan   Seoul   Singapore   Sydney   Toronto

The *McGraw·Hill* Companies

Copyright © 2003 by Vince Lombardi, Jr. All rights reserved.
Printed in the United States of America. Except as permitted under
the United States Copyright Act of 1976, no part of this publication
may be reproduced or distributed in any form or by any means, or
stored in a data base or retrieval system, without the prior written
permission of the publisher.

The photographs are used courtesy of Vernon J. Biever. Copyright
© Vernon J. Biever.

1 2 3 4 5 6 7 8 9 0 AGM/AGM 0 9 8 7 6 5 4 3 2

ISBN 0-07-139096-0

McGraw-Hill books are available at special quantity discounts to use
as premiums and sales promotions, or for use in corporate training
programs. For more information, please write to the Director of
Special Sales, Professional Publishing, McGraw-Hill, Two Penn
Plaza, New York, NY 10121-2298. Or contact your local bookstore.

 This book is printed on recycled, acid-free paper containing a
minimum of 50% recycled, de-inked fiber.

CONTENTS

ACKNOWLEDGEMENTS

The author and publisher would like to thank the Green Bay Packer Hall of Fame, especially Tom Murphy, for allowing us access to Vince Lombardi's papers and Vernon J. Biever for providing the photographs.

The author offers his sincere gratitude to McGraw-Hill publisher Jeffrey Krames not only for his vision but also for displaying his usual brand of can-do "Lombardi spirit." I would also like to thank the talented team of Jeff Cruikshank and Chloe Kline for their superb editorial and research assistance. And lastly, I acknowledge McGraw-Hill's Peter McCurdy and David Dell'Accio for helping to turn this book into a reality.

The Essential Vince Lombardi

INTRODUCTION

I love quotes.

Believe it or not, I have no fewer than thirty-one books of quotations on my bookshelf.

As a speaker and writer, I'm always finding that quotes come in handy when I am searching for a way to make a point. Sometimes they clarify my thinking on a certain concept. At other times I'm thrilled to find that someone has expressed the very idea for which I was trying to find the right words. Here are two quotes that illustrate my point:

I quote others only to better express myself.
                                    Herbert Gardner

The wisdom of the wise and the experience of the ages are perpetuated by quotes.
                                    Benjamin Disraeli

My father, Vince Lombardi, enjoyed quotes too. I think he would have been pleased to see his own words collected in a book of quotations. I also think he would have been somewhat surprised: What words of inspiration could *he* offer to the world at large outside of football?

I think this modesty would have been misplaced. It might be stretching a point to call my father eloquent, but I think anyone who knew him would agree that he spoke with urgency, passion, and *conviction*—and, as a result, with power. Today, some thirty years after his death, the power of that conviction still shines through the text of his speeches, letters, and other writings.

My father was an omnivorous reader to whom good ideas tended to stick. When the time came to express himself, he frequently called upon the great store of motivational nuggets he held in his head. Emerson, Byron, and MacArthur are only a few of the minds my father turned to for inspiration.

This wasn't just a pastime or an intellectual pursuit. It was his *business*. When you have to motivate a large group of young men every day for six months, you have to look for all the help you can get ... and from any source you can lay your hands on.

If you're already a Vince Lombardi fan, you'll probably find some quotes in this book that you'll recognize, for example, "Winning isn't everything, it's the only thing." You will also find out some interesting information about such legendary quotes. For example, my father was not the first to make that controversial assertion, although it will forever be associated with his name!

In fact, wherever helpful, I've included my own commentaries on my father's words and ideas. In some cases I've tried to correct what I take to be a general misconception of what my father was trying to express. In other cases I've provided background to make a quote more understandable. (I've included a short biographical essay after this introduction for the same reason.) And in a few cases I've confessed that I'm not exactly sure *what* my father was trying to say. "Powerful" does not always translate into "clear."

In the following pages you will also find many new thoughts and ideas based on a recent review of my father's papers at the Green Bay Packer Hall of Fame. Of course, I've included excerpts from his most carefully worked out speeches. But I've also included some candid and unstudied remarks, mostly from interviews, that provide insight into his thinking. In addition, I've included a couple of quotes from other individuals who knew, understood, and respected my father. Finally, I've included commentaries provided by my sister Susan, who has her own unique perspective on Dad's thoughts on life and leadership and was kind enough to review this work.

A final story about quotations in the Lombardi households: One year for Christmas my wife and I gave my father a copy of *Bartlett's Familiar Quotations*. My father wasn't an easy person to buy a present for—he was a man of relatively simple tastes, and he eventually accumulated enough wealth to satisfy all of his material needs—so I was pretty proud of finding something that I was sure he would use. He seemed delighted with the gift.

So you can imagine my vexation when, shortly after Christmas, we discovered in his library a very well worn copy of *Bartlett's*. My father smiled his big grin when we confronted him with the evidence. Yes, he said, he had pretended that this was an exciting new resource, but only because he hadn't wanted to disappoint us. Well, I said to myself, at least I guessed right. At least it was something that he did find useful.

The following Christmas we got the better of him (which wasn't easy to do). We retrieved the pristine copy of *Bartlett's* from his library, wrapped it up, and—with perfectly straight faces—gave it to him again. I have a great picture of my father laughing uproariously as he opened that present.

I hope you will find inspiration in the ideas and thoughts contained in this book, as so many of my father's players and countless others have over the years.

To my father, coaching and teaching were synonymous. He believed it was his duty to teach his players not only how to be successful on the football field but also how to live happy, responsible, and successful lives.

He certainly did that for me. I hope that in some way this book will give you access to his wisdom and the wisdom of others he thought worth repeating.

A BRIEF BIOGRAPHY

This is in no sense in writing a biography of my father. But it may be helpful to provide some background information on my father's remarkable career in order to place some of the following quotes in context.

Vincent Thomas Lombardi was born on June 11, 1913, to an Italian-American family living in Sheepshead Bay, New York. Sheepshead Bay was a section of Brooklyn that had once been an upper-class summer resort area but had gradually been transformed into a haven for the immigrants pouring into the city through Ellis Island. His father and uncle ran Lombardi Bros., a successful wholesale meat venture, and young Vince got his first business education in the meat business.

My dad attended high school at Cathedral Prep, a school run by the Brooklyn Diocese for Catholic boys who hoped to become priests. He ultimately left

Cathedral for Saint Francis Prep, Brooklyn's oldest Catholic school, where he was able to play competitive football for the first time. The Church remained a central part of his belief system and his daily discipline for the rest of his life.

My father enrolled at Fordham University in the fall of 1933 on a football scholarship. Fordham was run by the Jesuit religious order. Those priests pushed him hard to think about the world and his place within it. Much of his belief in hard work and dedication to excellence can be traced directly to his Jesuit tutors.

My father played football at Fordham, though as it turned out, he was both injury-prone and not a particularly gifted athlete. But Fordham had good teams in the mid-1930s, and the offensive line (including my father, whose nickname in those years was "Butch") achieved regional celebrity as the "Seven Blocks of Granite."

My dad didn't want to work in the family meat business after college. He enrolled in Fordham's law school at his father's urging but abandoned that effort after a single semester. In the fall of 1939 he took a job at Saint Cecilia High School, a parochial school in Englewood, New Jersey, where a Fordham teammate hired him as an assistant football coach. (He also taught physics, chemistry, and Latin.) In 1940 he married my mother, Marie Planitz, and two years later I was born, on April 27, 1942.

That same year my father became head coach at "Saints," as Saint Cecilia's was fondly called, and began to build his reputation as a football coach. At one point the high school team ran off a string of thirty-two unbeaten games, an astounding accomplishment for such a small school. That success led to an assistant coaching position at his alma mater, Fordham, which he took up in the summer of 1947. A few months earlier my sister Susan was born, rounding out our family.

In January 1949 my father took yet another assistant position, this time at the United States Military Academy at West Point, where he worked for Colonel Earl H. "Red" Blaik, coach of the Army team. Blaik was another formative influence on my father. Blaik loved studying game film—a relatively unknown technique back in the late 1940s—and worked both his coaches and his players hard. He also had a gift for making complex things simple, another trait my father successfully assimilated.

In 1954 my father broke into the professional football ranks when he was offered an assistant coach position with the New York Giants. He had hoped to get the Giants' head coaching job but instead wound up as the offensive coordinator to Jim Lee Howell. This was a difficult but valuable learning experience for both my father and the Giants. To make a long story short, my father learned how to work with very gifted professional athletes and the athletes were introduced to his emphasis on discipline and hard work.

In 1957 the Philadelphia Eagles asked my father to take their head coaching position. It was tempting: It was one of only twelve such jobs in the world, and the other eleven were spoken for. But the Eagles were in disarray not only on the field but also off the field. After much hesitation he turned the Eagles down, hoping for an opportunity with a team with a better management structure.

That opportunity came in 1958, when one of the worst franchises in the NFL—the Green Bay Packers— asked my father to take over as their head coach. The once-proud Packers had just finished a miserable 1-10-1 season, the worst in the team's history. My dad signed on as coach and general manager, which effectively gave him complete operating control over the team.

The events of the next decade were nothing short of remarkable. The Packers enjoyed a winning season during my father's first year as head coach, and the team went on to win NFL titles in 1961, 1962, and 1965. They also took home the first two Super Bowl titles, in 1966 and 1967. My father's brilliance as a coach became legendary, and his fame quickly spread from Green Bay to the rest of the country.

In the years in which he served the Packers as both coach and general manager, his outside activities were limited to the occasional product endorsement and speaking engagement. At first he favored gatherings with which he felt some natural kinship, such as Catholic charitable organizations, but over time he accepted more offers to speak to organizations such as the National Organization of Manufacturers and other industry groups. His themes remained very consistent even as his platform got bigger. Many of the quotes contained in this book are taken directly from those speeches.

My father stepped down as the Packers' head coach at the end of the 1967 season, though he retained the general manager's job. Although he needed a break and a change, he soon realized that he had made a serious mistake. After a year of self-imposed idleness he surprised the football world by announcing that he had agreed to serve as the head coach of the Washington Redskins, a team run by the celebrated lawyer Edward Bennett Williams.

The Redskins were a distressingly average team, having played .500 ball for a dozen years. They had not won a championship for almost thirty years. Once again, as he had a decade earlier in Green Bay, my dad turned things around, mostly through the force of his personality and the heroic efforts of a small group of talented players who understood and bought into the Lombardi method. Together, they led the team to a respectable 7-5-2 record in the 1969 season.

As it turned out, it was my father's last campaign. He was taken ill in the spring of 1970 and was hospitalized in June with intestinal distress. The grim diagnosis: a virulent cancer of the colon. He died on September 3, 1970, and the football world—and a good piece of the larger world as well—felt the loss.

Coming off the field after a win,
although you wouldn't know it looking at his face.

ABILITY

Ability in the league is more or less equal—you are no better or worse than any other player or team in the league. The real difference lies in other things besides ability.

This statement may seem surprising coming from the coach of one of the most talented teams of its era, but the fact is that my father was not the most skilled football player. He made up for it, however, with other qualities: courage, desire, determination, grit, and hard work. He looked for the same attributes in his players.

Not that talent or ability wasn't important. My father recognized and sought talented players and brought as many as he could to Green Bay. But equally important to him was what the players did with that ability, and this is where the notion of responsibility comes in. My father believed that those with the ability to do great things had a duty to use that ability, a responsibility to develop that ability and become the best they could be.

Take Paul Hornung. Hornung was ready to retire when my father arrived in Green Bay. He was disillusioned with the team's failure and his own disappointing seasons with the Packers. Coming out of Notre Dame, the Heisman Trophy winner had done very little as a pro to justify the honor. My father, after watching tapes of the Packers, knew Hornung was a player with great potential. "When I joined this club in 1959," he later said, "Paul Hornung was more celebrated for his reputed exploits off the field than on, but after the months I had spent studying the movies of Packer games, I knew that one of the ballplayers I needed was Paul Hornung."

With the right coaching, in other words, Hornung could be a star. My father made it clear to Hornung what he expected from him, and put him to work. And the results speak for themselves: Hornung went on to be the NFL scoring leader three years in a row and was subsequently inducted into the Pro Football Hall of Fame.

Ability involves responsibility; power to its last particle is duty.

ADVERSITY

My father's success as a coach eventually led to speaking engagements in which he addressed business and industry leaders. He often peppered his talks with quotes from inspirational figures from his own life. Sometimes this meant the Jesuit teachers who first schooled him in duty, sacrifice, and self-denial. Sometimes it meant one of the many authors he had read and reread in his years of schooling. Often he would subtly alter the quotations to better fit his own purposes. For example, he loved to quote Lord Byron, "Adversity is the first path to truth." Sometimes this would appear verbatim in one of my father's speeches. At other times it would become something more fitting to his audience: "Adversity is the first path to a championship."

Sometimes it's good to have an obstacle to overcome, whether in football or anything. When things go bad, we usually rise to the occasion.

A team, like men, must be brought to its knees before it can rise again.

Whatever the reasons, the fact that I did not get the coaching opportunities I felt I deserved motivated me greatly.

My father's career developed slowly, something that caused him anxiety for a number of years. In 1948 it was rumored that he would be the next head coach at Fordham, where he had been the assistant coach for two years, but that job never materialized. Then, both at West Point and with the New York Giants, he watched from the sidelines as other coaches of equal or lesser ability got jobs he didn't get. I think he came close to giving up hope, and I certainly think he resigned himself to being an assistant coach for the rest of his career. But ultimately, when he got the break in Green Bay, he was able to use all the frustration of his missed opportunities to motivate him toward success.

Let it be an example to all of us. The Green Bay Packers are no better than anyone else when they aren't ready, when they play as individuals and not as one. . . . Our greatest glory is not in never failing but in rising every time we fall.

This is taken from my father's postgame talk to the Packers after a humiliating Thanksgiving Day loss to the Detroit Lions in 1961. The last sentence quotes Ralph Waldo Emerson. This quotation was one of his favorites and found its way into many different motivational speeches. If football was a crusade to him, it was inevitable that sometimes he would lose a battle. But true victory was in recovering from the setback and going on to win the next game.

We must have a balanced attitude toward life's problems. We must face certain humiliations and frustrations in ourselves. We must experience failure and disappointment. We must expect trials and tragedies and accept them without bitterness.

This statement is classic Roman Catholic teaching—his seminary training shining through.

We want to perfect ourselves so that we can win with less struggle and increasing ease, but the strange thing is that it's not the easy wins we ostensibly seek but rather the difficult struggles to which we really look forward.

ASPIRATIONS

I believe in what Robert Browning said—that "reach should always exceed the grasp." I have heard two responses given to the man who was always reaching for the moon—the

first, that even if you do not reach the moon, you will perhaps grab a star or two. The other answer is that the man who keeps reaching for the moon will sooner or later strain himself. I tend to believe in catching stars.

I tend to believe in catching stars and have been willing to take my chances on the hernia.

AUTHORITY

You gotta remember one thing: If you're going to exercise authority, you've got to respect it.

My father is quoted here by Jim Kensil, assistant to the NFL commissioner, on an occasion when he (reluctantly) agreed to skip seeing his parents in favor of a New York press conference that wasn't on his calendar and that he didn't want to attend. This quote says a lot about him; it reflects a deeply held belief in the importance of respecting authority. This was a result of his seminary training, his Jesuit training, and his coaching days at West Point.

My father didn't usually challenge authority. On one occasion, however—after a Washington Redskins game characterized by some tough calls—he followed the game officials into their dressing room to continue arguing over their decisions. This kind of behavior was strictly against league rules. Commissioner Pete Rozelle didn't fine my father but sent him a letter expressing shock at his behavior, especially given my father's views on the importance of respecting authority. The letter was far more effective than a fine would have been. In any case, my father was deeply embarrassed by the whole incident.

A disciplined person is one who follows the will of the one who gives the orders.

Ray Nitschke ran over everyone who got in his way,
including Coach Lombardi on this play along the Packer sideline.

BAD APPLES

I don't want any bad apples in my organization. I get one [bad] apple in the bushel over here, and the rest of them will start rotting, too.

Dominic Olejniczak, the president of the Packers, is quoting my father here, explaining why he got rid of a player with a poor attitude. The player was a wide receiver, an all-Pro and a very talented player, and the Packers didn't have enough talented players at that time. But he was a griper and a complainer, and he rarely gave 100 percent. I don't think he *ever* stepped onto the practice field; my father traded him during the off-season. This was partly motivated by personnel needs, but it was also calculated. It sent a message: "Play my way, respect my authority, and give me everything you've got. Or find another team."

BEST, DOING ONE'S

Bart Starr to Lombardi: Your consistent unwillingness to settle for anything less than excellence will always serve as an inspirational beacon for all of us who played for you.

If you settle for nothing less than your best, you will be amazed at what you can accomplish in your life.

People want to excel. That's a human constant.

I have always believed that every man's personal commitment ought to be toward excellence.

Striving for excellence was a lesson that my father drilled into our family again and again. When I was in high school, my father had no tolerance for any slip in my grades. If one was apparent—and it often was—I was immediately grounded until the next report card came out.

Later, my father more or less forbade me from pursuing a career as a football coach. In his mind, he wanted something better for me: He wanted me to be a lawyer.

My father didn't let up after high school, either. During my sophomore year at Saint Thomas College (now the University of Saint Thomas) in Saint Paul, I tried to rent an off-campus apartment with several friends. When my father heard about it, he called the dean and insisted that I move back to the dorm or be sent home, and within a week I was back in the dorm.

And each summer during my high school and college years my father would arrange backbreaking summer jobs for me either in construction or loading semis and boxcars with containers of pickles and vinegar. He never tried to find me an easy job, and I think he was making a point here. If I had had any doubts about going to college, those summer jobs made it clear to me that I didn't want the alternative.

I chafed under the tight restrictions that he placed on me. Often I ignored his advice (my first attempt at law school lasted only about two months because I was going to law school for his reasons, not mine). But in many ways he knew me better than I knew myself. After all, he had been dealing with young men his entire career. After that first failed attempt, I returned to law school the following year, earning my degree at night—and I'm glad that I did. And the college apartment? Several of my fellow renters dropped out of college altogether, no doubt too distracted by the freedoms they enjoyed off campus. My father was a taskmaster, but there was a method behind it. He knew that I could succeed, and he wouldn't take no for an answer.

> **Once, in Green Bay, I started talking on the theme that the Lord gave us certain talents, and if we don't use those talents to their fullest, we're cheating—cheating on the Lord, and cheating on ourselves. I bet I talked 15, 20 minutes on that subject.**

BUSINESS

Business is a very complex machine, all of whose components are people, and as in a football team, it is vital that people mesh and gear smoothly.

Most people in business possess a leadership ability. Unfortunately, leadership does not rest solely upon ability and capacity. That is not enough. A man must be willing to use it.

Public acceptance is vital to the original success and the continuing success of any business. No matter how popular or successful at the moment or how rosy the future appears, the public acceptance of any kind of product must be deserved to be kept. There is no room for complacency in this regard.

Every business has an image created in the minds of the people it serves. There is absolutely no escaping this fact. Therefore, the management must first decide what image it wants created, then must engage in self-analysis to see what actual image exists, and then must constantly have a sensitivity and awareness about the factors that will keep the proper image or destroy it.

In handling that pigskin or in handling a product, both of us are looking for the same thing—the pleasing of our customers and winning and keeping their loyalty.

Coach Lombardi was always very animated on the sidelines.

CAMARADERIE

There's a great *closeness* on a football team, you know—a rapport between the men and the coach that's like no other sport. It's a binding together, a knitting together. For me, it's like fathers and sons, and that's what I missed. I missed players coming up to me and saying, "Coach, I need some help because my baby's sick." Or, "Mr. Lombardi, I want to talk with you about trouble I'm having with my wife." That's what I missed most. The closeness.

This statement is an almost universal emotion expressed by almost every player and coach involved in a team sport. The closeness of his team was incredibly important to my father, and it was one of the things that he missed when he stopped coaching the Packers and became the general manager. It was most likely a factor in his decision to take the Washington Redskins job.

You never really let go of these guys, you know. I just heard the other day about a kid I used to coach in high school. I heard he's in trouble. I heard he's doing a lot of heavy drinking. It's corny and it'll sound awful in writing, but you just feel bad when you know you couldn't get through to a kid like that.

CAUTION

You must forget about being cautious, because if you don't you're licked before you start.

CHANGE

Changes take time. They do not take place overnight.

Another question I'm asked over and over: "What happens during half-time in the locker room?" Actually, not much. You are on a game plan. You have analyzed your

opponents as a unit and as individuals, structured your battle strategy around what you believe to be their weaknesses—and you are committed. . . . Now, here you are in the heat of combat and somehow your plan isn't working. Why? You try to find out during the half. Usually, we come out with a slight modification, seldom a radical change. You've been geared to play it one way. You're pretty much stuck with it. The more experienced a unit you are, the more you are attuned to your teammates, the more synchronized you are to each other—even in slightly modified changes—the better chance you have of coming back to win.

This is an interesting paradox that appears time and again throughout my father's comments. The more disciplined and highly trained you are, the easier it is to make changes. Discipline and training don't necessarily lead to rigidity; in certain cases they can actually create flexibility.

CHARACTER

Football is a game in which winning cannot be accomplished except by complete dedication.

It is a game in which winning requires sacrifice. These are two great attributes toward the building of character.

Character, rather than education, is a man's greatest need and man's greatest safeguard, because character is higher than the intellect.

My father is quoting Herbert Spencer here, a quote which became a favorite theme over the years. Education was important to my father: He taught high school physics, chemistry, and Latin for many years, and if he hadn't made a life of coaching, which to him was teaching, there's no doubt that he would have made a life in some sort of a classroom. But he always recognized that there were types of knowledge more important than book learning and that developing character was as crucial to society as imparting an education.

The place of character, like that of God, is everywhere.

To be honest, I'm not entirely sure what my father was getting at with this statement. I think it probably reflects his belief in the importance of letting character lead daily life. It's not enough for character to show itself in moments of crisis; it's something that must be practiced daily.

If you would create something, you must be something.

You can't just dream yourself into character. You must hammer, you must forge one out for yourself.

Improvements in moral character are our own responsibility. Bad habits are eliminated not by others, but by ourselves.

"Character is the result of two things: mental attitude and the way we spend our time." (quoting Elbert Hubbard)

Throughout my father's speeches you will see a common theme: You have to be yourself. This quotation, which is one expression of that idea, appeared frequently in my father's speeches. He would also modify it, combining it with another of his favorite ideas: working to develop your own character: "Character is the direct result of mental attitude, and you cannot copy someone else's particular character qualifications but must develop your own according to your particular personality."

CHARISMA

How can I describe my father's charisma? It was a quality that nobody who met him would question, though he himself downplayed the notion. He had that mysterious ability to inspire, to walk into a roomful of men and make them uncomfortable, to make them pull in their stomachs, stand up straight, and put their drinks out of sight.

His ability wasn't unstudied: My father believed that you had to work at this just as you did in putting together a game plan. Several times during my childhood I walked into his office or his locker room to find him standing at the mirror and trying out different expressions. He knew the effect of a well-timed smile or scowl and wanted to be able to call up precisely the right expression at precisely the right moment.

If you take all twenty-six coaches in pro football and look at their football *knowledge*, you'd find there's almost no difference. So if the knowledge isn't different, what's different? The coach's personality. See? Now, how am I supposed to explain my own personality? What am I supposed to say? That I'm a great leader? A mental powerhouse? That I've got *charisma*?

COACHING

My father had a coaching method particular to his personality. While he expected his assistant coaches to challenge him, it was always clear who was in control. He wanted them to speak up, but he didn't expect them to discipline players on the field. I can recall a couple times when one coach yelled at a player and my father told him, "That's my job." He wanted feedback from the coaches in the coaches' meetings, yet he had the final say. This again is a common theme throughout his career.

In coaching you speak in cliches, but I mean every one of them.

The only way I know how to coach this game is all the way.

A great measure of a coach's success is determined by how well he makes himself understood to the players.

To be the coach of a great football team, you've got to be a good teacher. "Molder" might be a better word. The team must be molded into a unit, must have a character absolutely of its own, without in any way

affecting the enormous value of personal aggressiveness of pride.

You can't coach without criticizing, and it's essential to understand how to criticize each man individually. For instance, some can take constructive criticism in front of a group, and some can't. Some can take it privately, but others can only take it indirectly. Football is a pressure business, and on my teams I put on most of the pressure. The point is that I've got to learn forty ways to pressure forty men.

Great coaches and great leaders know their people well enough to motivate each one differently. To try to motivate everyone the same way is the mark of a lazy leader.

Max McGee on Lombardi: He was the greatest psychologist.

[Five-time all-pro defensive tackle] Henry Jordan has a tendency to be satisfied, which is why I don't flatter him much, and why often, when we're reviewing the pictures, I make him a target. Sometimes you will make a man a target to impress somebody else who can't accept public criticism, but I will

call Hank because we both know his ability and know that I'm on him to bring it out, and because he performs best when he's just a little upset.

In the first year at Saint Cecilia we naturally made the same mistake everyone does. We tried to give them too much. It was the first time, too, that I truly realized that a ball club is made up of as many different individuals as there are positions on it, that some need a whip and others a pat on the back, and others are better off when they're ignored, and that there are limitations imposed by the difference in physical ability and mentality. The amount that can be consumed and executed by a team is controlled by the weakest man on it, and while others can give him physical help, he has to do his own thinking.

It's no damn fun being hard. I've been doing this for years and years and years. It's never been great fun. You have to drive yourself constantly. I don't enjoy it. It takes a hell of a lot out of me. And Christ, you get kind of embarrassed with yourself sometimes. You berate somebody, and you feel disgusted with yourself for doing it, for being in a job where you have to.

No carrot and stick for me. I'll never look for a way to make it up to a guy I've been on. That doesn't mean I won't push some people more than others. You've seen me on the field, and there are obviously people I push all the time and some I don't. There are many people here it took me a longer time to find out how far I could push, don't know yet what their limit is. I'll be pushing them all over again next year until I do find their limit.

By the same token, there are some people I knew I couldn't push. Some people I had doubts about, and I pushed them and berated them to find out what I could about their character, their limits. Those are the things that are important to me, because this is what the game is all about.

COMMITMENT

Introducing Wisconsin Senator Gaylord Nelson: The quality of life is a full measure

of personal commitment, whether it's to football, or business, or government.

Commitment was one of my father's favorite themes. Among the virtues that he felt were necessary for a winner, commitment was first among equals. A winner must be committed to discipline, committed to sacrifice and self-denial, and committed to hard work.

I don't know how else to live. Unless a man believes in himself, and makes a total commitment to his career, and puts everything he has into it—his mind, his body, and his heart—what's life worth to him?

Once a man has made a commitment to a way of life, he puts the greatest strength in the world behind it. Something we call "heart power." Once a man has made this commitment, nothing will stop him short of success.

In order to succeed, this group will need a singleness of purpose, they will need a dedication, and they will have to convince all of their prospects of the willingness to sacrifice.

COMMON SENSE

I like to have a player who possesses common sense and the ability to transmit that common sense to others.

COMPETITION

My father equated competition with what made America great. He believed that the virtues and qualities learned through competitive athletics were the very qualities needed to succeed in life, and he encouraged parents and institutions to place more emphasis on competitive sports. He practiced what he preached: When he was a high school coach, he frequently made a speech entitled "I'm Raising My Son to Be an Athlete."

> **Those of you who are fathers and have sons and would have them grow into [leaders], have them play a game.**
>
> **The number one aim of all the [military] academies is the development of leaders, and the academies have found that they do this best through competition in athletics.**
>
> **Brains without competitive hearts are rudderless.**

In my father's mind, this statement applied to institutions as well as individuals. One of his favorite sayings was "A college or a university without a football team is nothing more than a medieval study hall."

COMPLEXITY

When my father first joined the NFL, the belief was that it was impossible to sustain a running game in the pros because the defenses were too big and strong. In fact, coaches liked the passing game because it was easier to coach, in that it involved the coordination of only a few people—the quarterback and receivers—and not the entire offensive eleven. My father's ability to coordinate the entire offense changed the way pro football was played in the 1960s.

What it comes down to is that to have a good running game, you have to like to run as a coach. You have to derive more creative satisfaction from the planning and the polishing of the coordination of seven or eight men rather than two or three.

I do not believe that this game is as complex as many people think it is and as some try to make it. At the same time, I don't think it's

as simple as it was twenty years ago. We try to make it as uncomplicated as we can . . . but we can't make it quite as simple as playground tag.

CONCENTRATION, POWERS OF

To my father, everything—and I mean everything—boiled down to one overriding question: How do I make this team better today than it was yesterday? He became so focused on this goal that anyone from his secretary, to the fans, to other coaches, to the press could be an intrusion if they happened to be guilty of bad timing and appeared at the wrong moment. He could be very abrupt at those times. It happened so often that he became very good at chasing people down the hall and apologizing.

Success in life is a matter not so much of talent or opportunity as it is concentration and perseverance.

CONFIDENCE

You defeat defeatism with confidence, and confidence comes from the man who leads. You just have it. It is not something you get. You have to have it right here in your belly.

One of my Dad's great strengths was that he had such great confidence—in his methods, in the way he prepared, and in his system—that the players couldn't help picking up on that confidence. He intended that his attitude would be picked up and adopted by the team. In other words, if he was somewhat defeatist or had doubts, they would pick up on it, would adopt it, and would go into a game feeling the same way.

Because of this, he kept any doubts he may have had to himself and made a brave show of complete confidence to the press and to his players. "We're going to have a winner the first year," he told reporters at the first press conference in Washington after he was named head coach of the Redskins.

Behind the scenes, however, this wasn't always the case. Years earlier, when he arrived in Green Bay and started studying some Packer films, he said to his secretary, Ruth McCloskey, "I think I have taken on more than I can handle. Will you pray for me and help me?"

Confidence is contagious. So is lack of confidence.

The man who is trained to his peak capacity will gain confidence. Confidence is contagious, and so is a lack of confidence.

You'd be surprised how much confidence a little success will bring.

This was certainly true for Bart Starr, the Packers' quarterback. Before my father went to Green Bay, the word on Bart Starr was that he didn't perform well under pressure or throw well enough to be a professional quarterback. My father watched tapes of Starr and studied him on the field. He realized that Starrr had the ability but lacked confidence. Once my father took him in hand and put a couple of successes under his belt, Starr became a Hall of Fame player and leader.

To play with confidence, a team must feel that everything possible has been done to prepare it fully for the coming game and there is nothing more we can tell them.

My dad realized that consistency in preparation and delivery is critical to a team's confidence. He wouldn't depart from his philosophy or system at the first sign of trouble. If he did, a player would ask himself, "What have we been doing up until now? Lombardi must not have much confidence either in us or in his system if he's going to radically change gears on us. Either we've been wasting our time up until now and/or he's lost confidence in himself or us."

On the other hand, my father was also careful not to let his players get too confident. In *Run to Daylight*, a book he wrote with W. C. Heinz in 1963, recounting a week in the life of the Packers, he tells of his mixed feelings when he read the headline "Pack Unstoppable" after an overwhelming win over the Bears. "Is that what I want?" he wonders. "I want them to believe in themselves, to believe that they can beat anyone, but just because we beat the crippled Bears 49 to 0, I don't want us strutting and spreading overconfidence."

My father was careful in these situations to build up the opposing team to the point where the players felt that it would be a tough game and that they needed to be totally prepared. It's a tricky balance: You don't want the players thinking that the opposition is better than they are, yet you don't want to create doubt in your players' minds.

Take this speech, made later in the same week to his team: "That was a fine performance on Sunday. They were hurt, but it was still your finest game this year. This was the first time you played a complete game without mistakes. I mean mistakes like penalties that stop us. I don't mean mistakes on plays. This is what it takes to win in this league, but you have to do it week after week. You have to knock off the contenders week after week, and you've got a big one this week."

A team that thinks it's going to lose *is* going to lose.

We are going to win some games. Do you know why? Because you are going to have confidence in me and my system.

You defeat defeatism with confidence.

I hold it more important to have the players' confidence than their affection.

I might add that this was his approach as a parent, as well, though in the case of our family, you might substitute "respect" for "confidence."

All the world loves a gambler . . . except when he loses.

CONTROL

I know a lot of great players that I cut not because they couldn't play football but because they weren't made for my system.

You mean, a one-man operation sort of thing. Yeah, I like that. That's one of the things that make it interesting. It's a $5 million business, and there are very few

positions that big where one man has so much say-so. Can put his own stamp on things. I like that.

Of course, $5 million is not a lot of money today, but it was back in the early 1960s, when my father made this comment about being the operating head of a football franchise.

If I were coaching and someone else in the organization were questioning me, I couldn't take that.

Once I got very hot under the collar after the quarterback ignored my suggestion when his call resulted in an interception. Of course, other times, where my play was not used but he was successful, I didn't make much of a fuss about it.

The leader must always walk the tightrope between the consent he must win and the control he must exert.

It took me a long time to understand this quote, but if you think about it, isn't this the essence of leadership?

You can call me a dictator. The fact is that I am reluctant to take any step that doesn't

have the wholehearted support of my whole staff.

I want it understood that I'm in complete command. I expect full cooperation from you people [in the Packers' organization], and you will get full cooperation from me in return.

I have been hired to do a job without interference, and I don't expect to have any.

My father had a simple concept of control. First, he figured out the things that he could control. Then, among those things, he focused on the ones that really determined the team's success. He controlled everything he thought had to do with the results on the field and left the ticket sales to someone else.

Of course, there were parts of the game where he had to give up control. For example, he had little to do with the defense. In fact, he really didn't know a whole lot about what the defense was doing. This accounts for one of his favorite phrases, often heard on the sidelines when the Packer defense was on the field: "What the hell is going on out there?" As a leader, you can't control everything, which is why my father made sure he had good people coaching his defense.

The control that the Packers afforded him was definitely a large part of my father's decision to take the job in Green Bay. He had been offered a position with the Philadelphia Eagles the year before but eventually turned it down for this very reason: He wouldn't have had complete control.

You cannot be successful in football—or in any organization—unless you have people who bend to your personality. They must bend or already be molded to your personality. I know damned well I can't coach all 640 players in the league. I'm only one man. I can only be that one man, and I've got to have men who bend to me.

CORNINESS

A lot of what I say sounds corny out of context. It's better in the heat of the moment. But it is *me*.

If you got my father going, he could really be corny; there are no two ways about it. But was that his problem, or is it ours? Take his words on "integrity" or "principles": They may sound idealistic or corny, but they're still what makes the world a safe, secure, and reasonable place to live. Without these attributes there can be no trust. Though some of my father's words may sound out of date and corny, that doesn't make them any less true.

CRITICISM

There's nothing personal about any of this. Any criticism I make of anyone, I make only because he's a ballplayer not living up to his potential. Any fine I levy on anyone, I levy because he's hurting not only himself but thirty-five other men.

A mature person profits from criticism.

Each of us . . . must develop a thick skin to criticism and let the caustic comments he receives from some quarters pass over his head. It is sometimes a hard thing to do, to ignore and even laugh at things that offend sensibilities.

My father did criticize! He made it into an art. The quote above indicates that a leader must have thick skin. It helps if that leader's followers have a thick skin as well.

I was certainly on the receiving end of a lot of his criticism. On Sunday mornings I would ride to the game with my father. Sometimes he would have seen my high school football game the day before, and he would spend part of the ride critiquing my effort. During my freshman year in high school I had a strange knee injury where I limped if I jogged, but if I ran hard, the knee didn't bother me. My father implied that he thought that I was faking the knee injury. I wasn't, and it hurt to hear him question me. Overall, however, in both high school and college, I took his criticism positively—after all, he did know something about the game of football!

*An early picture of a young Lombardi
and a younger Bart Starr.*

DEFEAT

Quoting Wendell Phillips: What is defeat? Nothing but education, nothing but the first step to something better.

Quoting Henry Ward Beecher: It is defeat that turns the bones to flint and gristle to muscle and makes men invincible and forms those basic natures that are now in ascendancy in the world. Do not be afraid of defeat.

These two quotations often found their way into my father's motivational speeches. I wonder if my father *had* to turn to other sources to find meaning in defeat because losing was so difficult for him. My father hated to lose, and—as noted previously—losing lost its sting for him only when the next "battle" eased the pain.

He hated to admit defeat. He often said, "When we lose a ballgame, it is only because time ran out on us. In other words, if we had enough time, we would have eventually won that ballgame." But it's also true that he learned more from his defeats than from his victories, however painful the process was. In preparing for games against a specific opponent, he would always spend more time studying the games that the Packers had lost to that team than the games the Packers had won against them. Finding and addressing every mistake that his team made gave him the best chance of not repeating the mistakes again.

How does a man meet his failures? That is the measure of the man. If he does not quit or curl up, he has the right stuff in him. Be a hard loser.

We want players who use defeat as a stimulus to tougher effort. You never find forty men who feel that way, but I'll take all I can get.

Defeat must be admitted before it is a reality.

Chuck Mercein (Packer and Redskin) on Lombardi: He refuses to accept defeat even

when he is defeated. I think he really believes that if the game goes on for another five minutes, he can win. It makes a difference to play under a guy like that, I can tell you.

DEFENSE

My father focused on the offensive side of the ball, and so the defensive coaches pretty much ran their own show. Offensively, he wanted feedback, but the final decision was his. As an offensive coach, however, he understood that you first build the team on defense. During the first several months with the Packers he often commented that there was nothing that would destroy a team's confidence more than to have the other team marching up and down the field at will. The Packers were always strong defensively, which was key, because sometimes they would go into a slump offensively. There were many times when they'd win low-scoring games by only a small margin.

Our primary need was for defensive help, because there is nothing more demoralizing to a whole squad than to see the opposition running roughshod over you.

DEPENDENCY

A football team's relationship to its coach isn't too far removed from that of a father to his family. Discipline, a discipline of love like that given by a father or mother, is not a hard thing to accept.

Our leaders no longer understand the relationship between themselves and the people; that is, the people want to be independent and dependent, all at the same time, to assert themselves and at the same time be told what to do.

My father's views on dependency shifted during his life. Take, for example, the two following quotes. The first statement was made early in his coaching career, the second after he had lived through the vast social changes of the 1960s.

Most everyone wants to be dependent. There are those who demand independence and need it, but I feel most people want discipline, and they'll take it so long as it's delivered within the spirit of teaching.

Great changes have taken place in the country in the last ten years. It's the nature of the times that there's more of a tendency to question now than there was ten years ago. The father complex is not around anymore.

DESIRE

I'd rather have a player with 50 percent ability and 100 percent desire because the guy with 100 percent desire you *know* is going to play every day so you can make a system to fit into what he can do. The other kind of guy—the guy with 100 percent ability and 50 percent desire—can screw up your whole system, because one day he'll be out there waltzing around.

The game is usually won by the team with the greatest desire.

Desire is that something inside a man that makes him determined that every one of the spectators will leave the stadium after a game convinced they have seen the best halfback ever in action.

There are physical exams that first night [of training camp]. There are six doctors, each behind a desk with the sign identifying his department. 1. History. 2. Heart-Lungs. 3. Dental. 4. Blood Pressure. 5. Abdomen-Hernia. 6. Eye-Ear-Nose-Throat. And I wish there were another one: 7. Desire. You can't examine them for that, though, and it shows only under game conditions, or perhaps in contact work.

DISCIPLINE

In a football game, there are approximately 160 football plays, and yet there are only 3 or 4 plays which have anything to do with the outcome of the game. The only problem is, no one knows when those 3 or 4 plays are coming up. As a result, each and every player must go all out on all 160 plays.

A good leader must be harder on himself than on anyone else. He must first discipline himself before he can discipline others. A man should not ask others to do things he

would not have asked himself to do at one time or another in his life.

What we do on some great occasion will probably depend on what we are; and what we are will depend on previous years of self-discipline.

My father is quoting H. P. Liddon here. This concept relates to my father's belief about character—that thoughts lead to words, words lead to actions, actions lead to habits, and habits make character. You have to work to develop your character, and in the end your character is formed by countless decisions that you make over the years of your life.

Discipline follows the same idea. Anyone can be disciplined for a day, but when the real test comes, it is the person who has been working and training for years who will have true command of his character.

Discipline is part of the will, really. A disciplined person is one who follows the will of the one who gives the orders. Also, you teach discipline by doing it over and over, by repetition and rote.

I think the nature of man is to be aggressive, and football offers a violent expression of that

fact. But to me, the violence is one of the great things about the game, because a man has to learn control. He's going in to knock somebody's block off—not in anger, but because that is his assignment. I don't know of any other place that demands such discipline.

It is easy to have faith in yourself and have discipline when you're a winner, when you're number one. What you've got to have is faith and discipline when you're not yet a winner.

Truly, I have never known a really successful man who deep in his heart did not understand the grind, the discipline it takes to win.

I sometimes wonder whether those of us who love football fully appreciate its great lesson: that dedication, discipline, and teamwork are necessary to success.

You don't do things right once in a while. You do them right all the time.

Quoting General Patton: There is only one kind of discipline: perfect discipline.

These words were a hallmark of my father's beliefs. He quoted Patton frequently both to his players and in his

speeches to business leaders. It's a phrase that he probably heard frequently during his West Point days, and
possibly the concept originally came to him from his
Jesuit teachers.

> **There is only one kind of discipline: perfect
> discipline. If I do not enforce and motivate
> discipline, then I am a potential failure in my
> job.**

> **There is only one kind of discipline, and that
> is perfect discipline. You, as a leader, must
> enforce and maintain that discipline; other-
> wise, you are a potential failure at your job.**

> **Jerry Kramer on Lombardi: Of all the les-
> sons I learned from Lombardi, from all his
> sermons on commitment and integrity and
> the work ethic, that one hit home the hard-
> est. I've found in business that only 15 or 20
> percent of the people do things right all the
> time. The other 80 or 85 percent are taking
> shortcuts, looking for the easy way, either
> stealing from others or cheating themselves.
> I've got an edge, because whenever I'm
> tempted to screw off, to cut corners, I hear
> that raspy voice saying, "This is the right**

way to do it. Which way are you going to do it, mister?"

DUTY

Before I can embrace freedom, I should be aware of what duties I have.

What amazes me is that so many Americans who acquire rights and privileges no other nation offers simply by accident of birth are utterly indifferent to the blessings bestowed upon them here. We cannot, we must not take these benefits for granted. They are precious endowments, but they are not free. For every right and freedom there is a corresponding duty and responsibility that we incur—to be good citizens, to obey our laws and uphold our constitution, to serve and defend our great country, and to exercise in full measure the very rights and privileges which are guaranteed to us.

We are our brother's keeper. I don't give a damn what people say. If people can't find work, whether it's their fault or not, you've got to help them and house them properly

and try to get rid of the conditions that have held them back.

It is our duty to be wary. We cannot abandon our responsibilities as citizens, as parents. Character is formed in the home, and we must be alert to the responsible task of molding it. We cannot abandon our duty to supervise our sons and daughters or to instill in them a moral fiber of the highest of ethical principles.

Somebody once tried to convince me that I was abused as a child. If they meant that I was physically disciplined if I broke a house rule, that's true. But I'll tell you, it didn't take me long to figure out that if I didn't break a rule, I wouldn't get disciplined. Cause and effect: You reap what you sow. This was an important lesson that I learned from my father, and I believe it's a lesson all parents should teach their children.

*As mentioned in the introduction,
quotes were everywhere in the Packer locker room.*

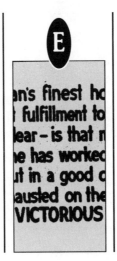

Ego

The ego destroys the humility in a person. Ego is what we think we are. The ego is the clamorous childness, the petulant childness, the spoiled childness.

Keep in mind that there are laws—independent of man's consent, ruling over reality, over nature, over man, too, whether he be willing to recognize them or not—to which we must bow, unless we think we can rule ourselves independently of the rest of nature. Egoism, in other words, must be defeated in self. The egoist is never happy.

EMOTION

Hell, I'm an emotional man. I cry. I cried when we won the Super Bowl, and I cried when I left Green Bay. I'm not ashamed of crying. Football's an emotional game. You can't be a cold fish and go out and coach. If you're going to be involved in it, you gotta take your emotions with you, mister.

I'll never give a game to an AFL team, and if you can't get emotional about what you believe in your heart, then you're in the wrong business.

My father is quoted by broadcaster Pat Summerall here, recounting an argument about the significance of preseason games between the well-established NFL and the newer AFL. He felt the competition between the leagues keenly, and it added to his desire to win during the first two "Super Bowl" contests.

He would, however, later regret a comment made after the first Super Bowl in which he said that any number of NFL teams could have beaten the AFL Kansas City Chiefs. "I said something to the press, and I wish I could get my words back. I told them that four or five NFL teams could have beaten Kansas City. It was the wrong thing to say, the wrong thing. I came off as an ungracious winner, and it was lousy." The lesson here is that while emotion and passion are important to success, they must be controlled.

I do have to build up an emotion before a game to do a good job. If I go out there feeling just fine about everything and everybody, I'm not doing the job I should.

EMPLOYEES

Our single most important public is our own employees—our team. For without a skilled, coordinated group of talented people behind us, we haven't a chance in the world of attaining success.

Just as in the business and manufacturing world, the members of a football team must constantly have their needs considered. Players think constantly of continuity and regularity of employment, adequate compensation and recognition, satisfactory working conditions, a sense of secure belonging, and pride in their work and organization.

ENERGY

My dad had more energy than a lot of people. If you have a clear, vivid, precise goal that you're passionate about, it gives you energy. But even then, I think there are some people who just innately have more energy. It's in their chemistry, their genes.

I think his energy came from both sources. I think some of it was just his chemistry and some of it was that he passionately believed in what he was doing. His energy was definitely part of what was compelling about him. His intensity was so obvious, it often seemed like he gave off sparks.

He got tired, and he got worn down, but come the next morning, he was ready to go. Again, part of it was his direction: He had a clear idea where he was going, what he wanted to do, and how he wanted to do it. He knew how to harness that energy productively. A lot of us have energy, yet we spend it destroying everything around us.

He periodically had to give himself a pep talk. Sometimes he would look for something just to tick him off so that he could get energized. He was a perfection-ist by nature, and when he saw imperfections, it would set him off. But that's where he got his energy. We all get our energy from different places. A lot of his energy

came from his anger. If you're going to be a perfectionist day in and day out, anger can be a pretty good way to
get yourself going. I sometimes feel it myself. Not only
anger but problems, dissonance. When I get mad at the
fax machine, I get a lot of work done right afterward, and
I bet that's true for a lot of people. But as a sole source
of energy it can be destructive, which in my father's case
may have something to do with the fact that he died at
age fifty-seven.

**The difference between success and failure
is energy.**

The difference between men is energy.

EXCUSES

**Don't succumb to excuses. Go back to the
job of making the corrections and forming
the habits that will make your goal possible.**

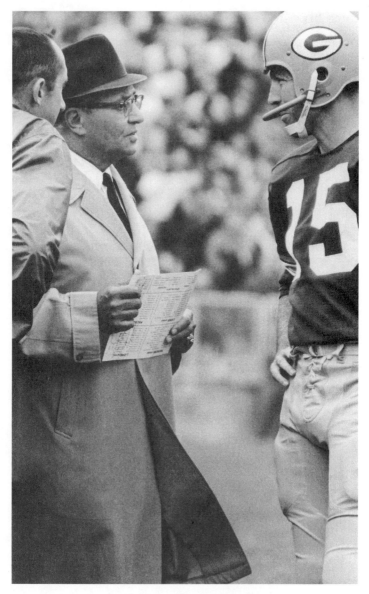

A sideline conference between
Coach Lombardi and his quarterback, Bart Starr.

FAILURE

It matters not how many times you fail—what matters is the successful attempt, which should be remembered, reinforced, and dwelt upon.

Errors, mistakes are the necessary steps in the learning process; once they have served their purpose, they should be forgotten. If we consistently dwell upon the errors, then the error or failure becomes the goal.

One of the first self-help books I ever read was *Psycho-Cybernetics* by Dr. Maxwell Maltz. It had a profound effect on me, and I was pleasantly surprised when I found a copy of the book—underlined and dog-eared—in my father's library after he passed away. I'm convinced that many of the concepts and ideas that formed my father's coaching philosophy—including focusing on the successful effort while putting an error quickly out of mind—came from his reading of *Psycho-Cybernetics*.

FAITH

One of the cornerstones of character is, of course, religion.

When we place our dependence in God, we are unencumbered, and we have no worry. In fact, we may even be reckless, insofar as our part in the production is concerned. This confidence, this sureness of action, is both contagious and an aid to the perfect action. The rest is in the hands of God—and this is the same God, gentlemen, who has won all His battles up to now.

I'm not afraid to meet my God now. But what I do regret is that there is so damn much left to be done on earth.

My father said this to a friend of his (who was a priest) while he lay dying in Georgetown Hospital. I don't believe he was talking about football when he commented about "so much being left to be done."

I derived my strength from daily communion.

We don't pray to win. We pray to play the best we can and to keep us free from injury. And the prayer we say after the game is one of thanksgiving.

My father's strength came from his faith. I'm not a theologian, and I don't pretend to understand the Jesuits all that well, but I think he picked up several key beliefs from them.

For example, the thought that we are imperfect, that we are fallen beings, that we all have a dark side that's in conflict with our better nature—I think my dad really subscribed to that and probably saw that working itself out within himself on a daily basis. I think my father was torn by the fact that his success, to a great degree, came from him being such a difficult and angry person. And I'm sure he struggled with it: "I yell, I chew out people, I demand, I push, and so on. I don't think that's totally right, but by golly, that's why I am who I am. That's why I am the success that I am."

Of course, that's not necessarily the image of Jesus Christ that we are familiar with. And that's why he went to church every day. His quarterback Bart Starr said it best:

"If you heard Coach Lombardi at practice every afternoon, you knew why he had to go to church every morning." I think he just felt it was a constant struggle, and going to mass, and prayer, helped him in that struggle.

My father was mostly very private about his religious beliefs. He taught Susan and me about his convictions mostly through example. We were never asked to attend daily Mass or pray the rosary or make outward demonstrations of our faith. We simply saw him do it. For someone with such deep-seated convictions, he was very hands-off. He also said relatively little to his players or to the media about his faith.

FALLIBILITY

I'm wrong just about as often as I'm right.

In dealing with people, the first thing we must have is all the facts, and then we must be constructive. If we are constructive, we will be reflecting our own sincerity and dedication, as well as our personal and company integrity. If the facts indicate we made a poor decision or took an improper action, then we must admit that we were wrong. On the other hand, if the evidence, based on those facts,

shows we were correct, we must stand firmly and fairly to what we believe is right.

FAME

Gentlemen, it is not true that I can walk across the Potomac River— not even when it is frozen.

These were my father's famous words to more than 100 reporters attending his first press conference as coach of the Washington Redskins.

I don't think Vince Lombardi is important enough to have a day set aside for him.

My father wrote these words to friends in Bergen County, New Jersey, who were trying to arrange a "Vince Lombardi Day." Celebrity presented a paradox to my father. Typically, people seek fame, or at least don't run from it. And at the appropriate time you bask in it. It wasn't quite that simple for my father.

He was terribly uncomfortable with fame. Although I think the idea appealed to him, he was also basically very shy and ill at ease with celebrity. He enjoyed his stature when he was among friends, but when it came to the general public, he was uneasy. He didn't like people interrupting his dinner. He didn't like people coming up to him in the bathroom, when he was standing at the urinal, and asking for his autograph. Who would?

As many people who actually experience celebrity know, the fame can get away from you, and you have to spend some time lowering people's expectations. This was particularly true when he made the move to the Redskins. There was immense pressure to create the same turnaround that he had in Green Bay, but it simply wasn't realistic. That last year he spent a lot of time trying to control the hype. He knew that in football, as in other walks of life, it wasn't very far from the penthouse to the outhouse.

FATIGUE

Fatigue and endurance are often thought of as physical obstacles, yet they are mental too. My father felt that young football players didn't get physically tired over the course of a long season, but they would get mentally tired. Unless they were disciplined and focused, unless they had bought into the one correct way of doing things—his way—when they felt fatigue and exhaustion, they would take shortcuts and make excuses.

Fatigue makes a coward of us all. When you're tired, you rationalize. You make

excuses in your mind. You say, "I'm too tired, I'm bushed, I can't do this, I'll loaf." Then you're a coward.

Sign on the locker room wall: Fatigue makes cowards of us all.

The Good Lord gave you a body that can stand most anything. It's your mind you have to convince.

Men in condition do not tire. High physical condition is vital to victory.

There is nothing you need be afraid of as long as you're aggressive and keep going. Keep going and you'll win.

FITNESS

Good physical condition is vital to success.

A man who is physically fit performs better at any job.

Beat your opponent physically. The team that wins consistently is the one in the best physical condition.

FOOTBALL, REFLECTIONS ON

You know why football is so popular? Those people running around hitting each other? Hell, no. It's because of the huddle. Every time the clock stops, every time the play is over, the huddle forms, and the fan puts himself in the same situation, tries to figure out what he would do. Football is *situation*, as much as action.

At many a moment on many a day, I am convinced that pro football must be a game for madmen, and I must be one of them.

A professional football team is a kind of community of displaced persons.

Football is a game of cliches, and I believe in every one of them.

The game, any game, played on a competitive level has become a symbol of this country's best attributes, namely courage, stamina, and coordinated efficiency.

Football is a hard-headed, cold business. No matter what a player did last year, if he can't do it this year, he has to go.

Football is a violent game. To play it any other way would be imbecilic. But because of its violent nature, it demands a personal discipline seldom found in modern life.

Football is a game of inches; and inches make the champion.

FREEDOM

Maybe we have too much freedom. Maybe we have so long ridiculed authority in the family, discipline in education, decency in conduct, and law in the state that our freedom has brought us close to chaos.

American freedom—and I mean freedom, not license—could be lost . . . unless the values underlying that freedom are thoroughly understood and embraced by our leaders.

FUMBLES

There's nothing you can do about fumbles except scream.

FUN

We don't encourage comedians. I don't want comic relief. The only way to keep football fun is to win. There is no laughter in losing.

You need an intelligent clown on a pro ball club.

My father made this comment about Fuzzy Thurston, a guard whose stellar pass protection for the Packers was matched by his tension-relieving antics. As my father wrote, "He has a talent for rhyming, and when he bellows out a calypso account of his personal heroics, he doesn't need a mike."

FUNDAMENTALS

Fundamentals were the foundation of my father's coaching philosophy. It was also about teamwork, and strategy, and all the other coaching points that come into play . . . but what it really comes down to is blocking and tackling. Fundamentals. At the ground level, this emphasis on fundamentals means you've got to take care of business, which is the guy lined up on your nose. This, in my father's mind, was the essence of football.

My father would drill the team in the basics over and over, preferring the perfection of one play to familiarity with a dozen. He started simple, and only when every player on the team had completely mastered one concept would he move on. He taught fewer plays but more options within each play. One year, after a difficult game in which the Packers struggled offensively, he started his lecture by saying, "Gentlemen, we're going back to the basics. This is a football." He was only half joking! Max McGee, from the back of the room, responded with his ready wit: "Coach, not so fast."

You never win a game unless you beat the guy in front of you. The score on the board doesn't mean a thing. That's for the fans. You've got to win the war with the man in front of you. You've got to get your man.

Every game boils down to doing the things you do best, and doing them over and over again.

The team that controls the ball controls the game.

In our business, the team that blocks best and tackles best is usually the team that wins the game.

There is an alarming tendency to stray away from the old basic of blocking, tackling, and avoiding mistakes. These are the salt and bread and butter of football. If you try to mix them with other fancy ingredients, you may miss out on your daily bread.

I believe that if you block and tackle better than the other team and the breaks are even, you're going to win.

Fundamentals win it. Football is two things; it's blocking and tackling. I don't care about formations or new defenses or tricks on defense. If you block and tackle better than the team you're playing, you'll win.

*The Packer offense being
introduced before a big game.*

GLORY

Every player must first place the team ahead of personal glory. The man who plays must make personal sacrifices—victory means team glory for everyone—personal glory means little if a team loses.

GOAL LINE

The goal line is where the moment of truth comes, and it is no place for a timid person.

How well you play defense on the goal line separates the champions from the people who just play football for lack of something else to do.

You find the real tough players on the goal line. You may never know the extent of a man's determination until he meets this separation point on the field.

The perfect illustration of this statement is Paul Hornung, the Packers' "Golden Boy." As my father wrote in *Run to Daylight*, "I have heard and read that Paul Hornung is not a great runner or a great passer or a great field-goal kicker, but he led the league in scoring for three seasons. What it comes down to is that in the middle of the field he may be only slightly better than an average ballplayer, but inside that twenty-yard line he is one of the greatest I've ever seen. He smells that goal line."

This quality of Hornung's stemmed from his overwhelming desire to win, his determination, his vision. These things were what endeared him to my father. Although Hornung had his faults, his willingness to work hard in practice and his unceasing desire to win created a bond with my father that remained unbroken even when Hornung was suspended from the league for a year for betting on games.

GROWTH, PERSONAL

The value of all our daily efforts is greater and more enduring if they create in each one of us a person who grows and understands and really lives. Or one who prevails for a larger and more meaningful victory—not only now but in time and, hopefully, in eternity.

When it rained, Coach Lombardi
didn't much care how he looked.

History, Value of

While statistics are interesting, they're all in the past.

It is something that you hate to do—to repeat a game plan or lift large portions of it—for two reasons. For one, you know your opponent hasn't forgotten where and how you hurt him, but more important, it makes you feel that you are losing whatever creativity you may have had.

It is the same every week. You spend days building for one opponent, and on Monday you have to forget it. Win or lose, if you don't put it behind you, you'll be wading around all week knee-deep in confusion.

HONESTY

In football and business, a leader must be honest with himself and the people he is working with. Skilled ignorance is often more powerful than knowledge and honesty—but only temporarily, only for a short time. In the long run, knowledge and honesty will pay off.

To be a leader, you must be honest with yourself and know, as a leader, you are like everyone else, only more so.

In football, as in anything else, if you alter your personality just to accomplish something you're not being true. You're being dishonest.

I never tell a football team anything that I don't absolutely believe myself. I always tell them the truth. I can't even try to deceive them, because I know they'd know. *I'd* know, so *they'd* know.

You have to sell yourself to them, to the group. And in order to sell yourself to the group, there is no way you can be dishonest about it. Therefore, what you sell has to come from the heart, and it has to be something you really believe in. That belief can be anything.

Faithfulness and truth are the most sacred excellences and endowments of the human mind.

HUMILITY

The finest compliment I can pay to [defensive tackle Henry Jordan] is that he is a humble man and knows the true relationship between God and man. He places his dependence upon God and he seeks His help, not just to win, but to do His will whenever it is presented to him.

Hero worship sometimes destroys the humility in a man. The ego, instead of the "I," becomes the dominant characteristic.

I'm humble, but I've never been overly modest.

I've always been a little confused by this off-the-cuff quote, and I'm not quite sure what he was trying to say. My guess is that my father knew that he was a pretty good coach, and when appropriate, he wanted credit for what he had accomplished. On the other hand, he knew that football was a team game and that ultimately the success he enjoyed was dependent on the efforts—sometimes the extraordinary efforts—of others. In addition, his religion taught him that he could accomplish very little without God's help.

*Before a game, here's Coach Lombardi
trying to influence a referee.*

Innovation

One must not hesitate to innovate and change with the times and the varying formations. The leader who stands still is not progressing, and he will not remain a leader for long.

Inspiration

Let us the leaders exert ourselves to fashion an image that none can criticize—that we ourselves are proud to view and that shall serve as a stunning example to our descendants.

I'm particularly fond of this quote, and I wish that more of today's leaders would follow its advice. If they did, the results for our society would be stunning.

When all is said and done, the leader must exercise an effective influence upon the people he leads. The degree to which he accomplishes this depends on the personality of the man: the incandescence of which he is capable, the flame that burns inside him, the magnetism which draws the hearts of other men to him.

Leadership is based on a spiritual quality, the power to inspire, the power to inspire others to follow. This spiritual quality may be for good or for evil. In many cases in the past, this quality has been devoted toward personal ends and was partly or wholly evil. Leadership which is evil, while it may temporarily succeed, always carries within itself the seeds of its own destruction.

INTEGRITY

If you cheat on the practice field, you'll cheat in the game. If you cheat in the game, you'll cheat the rest of your life. I'll not have it.

*Riding off the field on the shoulders of Jerry Kramer
after winning Super Bowl II.*

Kicking

In the closest football games, some part of the kicking game will be the deciding factor.

The kickoff is always a scary play, but there is equal nervousness on both sides.

Knowledge, of Others

I saw an ad in the paper recently, and I give you my oath it is true, and it leads me to another point—that advertisement read, "For sale, a complete set of encyclopedias, never used, wife knows everything." Well, no one knows everything, particularly about people.

No one knows everything, particularly about people. I'm not an expert in dealing with people. And I think we should all remember that none of us really is.

KNOWLEDGE, OF SELF

One of our goals in life has to be to know ourselves, as the ancient Greek axiom put it. It is the first step toward self-improvement.

Study yourself—not too much, though, and not to the neglect of your ordinary duties in life.

Every little knowledge about ourselves calls for corresponding endeavor for improvement.

Here is Coach Lombardi's classic look of dissatisfaction with what is happening on the field.

LEADERSHIP

As a football coach, as in other leadership positions, it's understood that you've got to persuade people to follow you. It's stated or implicit: "We're going to do it my way. It may not be the only way, but that's the way we're going to do it, because I'm the leader. I've been around longer, I know a little bit more than you do, and I've got a sense of the big picture. For good or ill, that's how it's going to be." In football, as in the military, this is somewhat easier to do because the people under your command don't have a lot of choices. But one way or another it has to happen: Either you cajole them, reward them, motivate them, and inspire them—or you threaten them.

It's worth noting, though, that my dad struggled with the fact that by staying in football, he didn't have as extensive a leadership impact as he might have liked. He was given consideration as a candidate for governor in Wisconsin and even mentioned as a vice-presidential possibility on the Nixon ticket in 1968 (until they learned that he was a Democrat). A reporter once asked him what he would do about violence on campus, if he were a university president. "If I could answer that one," he replied, "I wouldn't be coaching. I'd like to do something for this country. To lead, you don't exist in the abstract like I'm doing now."

In another conversation with Tom Dowling, the author of *Coach*, an insightful write-up of my dad's year with the Washington Redskins, my father added that he hesitated about running for office because he wasn't sure his personality was a good fit. "I wasn't sure I could take the beating you get in public life. At the same time, I liked to think I could make a contribution to people. You like to think you can rise to a new challenge. But I wasn't sure about those things."

Leadership rests not only on outstanding ability but on commitment, loyalty, pride, and followers ready to accept guidance.

Success is to be placed in a position of command, and the doctrine of command can be summed up in one word: leadership.

Successful people are leaders, and leadership is the ability to direct people, but more so, to have those people accept it.

Leadership is defined as the ability to direct people, but more important, to have those people accept direction.

Leadership, with the willingness to use it, is based upon truth and character. It must have truth in its purpose and willpower in its character.

The new leadership is in sacrifice, in self-denial. It is in love. It is fearlessness. It is in humility and it is in the perfectly disciplined will.

Leadership is not just one quality but rather a blend of many qualities, and while no one individual possesses all of the needed talents that go into leadership, each man can develop a combination to make him a leader.

What is needed in the world today is not just engineers and scientists but rather people who will keep their heads in an emergency and in every field: leaders, in other words, who can meet intricate problems with wisdom and with courage.

Leaders are made, and contrary to the opinion of many, they are not born. . . . They are made by hard effort, which is the price we must all pay for success.

Leadership ability should extend further than the management of your company.

You must believe that the group wants, above all else, for the leader to have a sense of approval and that once this feeling prevails, production, discipline, and morale will all be high. In return, from the group, you must demand cooperation to promote the goals of the corporation.

Leaders are lonely people and, whether cordial or remote in manner, are destined to maintain a certain distance between themselves and the members of the group.

A leader is judged in terms of what others do to obtain the results that he is placed there to get.

The commander alone is responsible for everything his unit does or fails to do and must be given commensurate authority. He cannot delegate his responsibility or any part of it; he may delegate a portion of his authority.

The leader does not exist in the abstract but rather in terms of what he does in a specific situation.

The strength of a group is in the strength of the leader. Many mornings when I am worried or depressed, I have to give myself what is almost a pep talk, because I am not going before that ball club without being able to exude assurance. I must be the first believer, because there is no way you can hoodwink the players.

LEARNING

All learning is trial and error.

The negative experiences do not inhibit, but rather contribute to, the learning process.

Errors and mistakes are the necessary steps in the learning process; once they have

served their purpose, they should be forgotten. If we consistently dwell upon the errors, then the error or failure becomes the goal.

If you learn from every mistake, you really didn't make a mistake.

This was advice my father gave to my sister, Susan. He really believed this, though he could be awfully hard on us when we did make mistakes. I think he thought he was accelerating the learning process!

LOMBARDI LEGEND

Dammit, I'm not a legend, because I don't want to be a legend. One main reason I came back to coaching is that I didn't want to be regarded as a legend. Because one, it's embarrassing as the devil, and two, you have to be [celebrated Chicago Bears coach George] Halas to be a legend. George Halas is seventy-four years old, and he's done something for the game. I'm too young to be a legend.

Nobody wants to be a legend, really.

My father has become a legend whether he wanted to be one or not. (If you read his words, he suggests pretty strongly that he didn't want this.) I think that part of this phenomenon is the fact that my dad died at an early age. If you look at other celebrated coaches, their feet of clay become evident at some point in their careers. That moment never came for my father.

If my father had lived and coached the Redskins to a series of unsuccessful seasons, I don't know if we'd be reading his words some thirty years later. Let's be honest: We tend to lionize people who go before their time. My dad could have developed his own feet of clay: The Redskins could have lost, he could have flown off the handle, or he could have antagonized the media more than he did. Any of these things would have been possible. And if any of them had happened, I might not be compiling a book of his thoughts.

The Redskin team turned out to be worse than he thought. He ended up having fewer talented players than he thought he was going to have, and the job was really going to turn into an uphill battle. The possibility of failure was real. (As it turned out, they went 7-5-2, their first winning season in years.) But his stint with the Redskins is perhaps the strongest argument that my father wasn't concerned with becoming a legend. If he had wanted to be thought of as a legend, why would he take on a team with so little talent?

During that year in Washington the two of us were riding in the car, and he turned to me and said, "You think I made a mistake taking this job, don't you?" To tell the truth, I hadn't thought about it one way or the other, but the question indicated to me that he had his own doubts.

LOSING

There is no laughter in losing.

We play every single game to win. In fact, there's only one way I can ever reconcile a loss. If every single man on that team knows when the game's over that he played the best ball game he was capable of, I can't fault him.

I don't want any good losers around here. If you think it's good to be a loser, give the other guy the opportunity.

Good losing is just a way to live with yourself, a way to live with defeat.

LOVE

Every year I try to think of a new word for Packer spirit. Last winter at the Super Bowl,

I called it something I have been sorry about ever since. When those tough sportswriters asked me what made the Packers click, I said, "Love." It was the kind that means loyalty, teamwork, respecting the dignity of another—heart power, not hate power.

Heart power is the strength of this world, of America, and hate power is the weakness of the world.

Everybody can like somebody's strengths and somebody's good looks. But can you like somebody's weaknesses? Can you accept him for his inabilities? That's what we have to do. That's what love is. It's not just the good things.

LOYALTY

I won't tolerate anything less than complete loyalty. Contrary to what you may have heard, I *will* tolerate practically everything else.

Loyalty is the very heart of the Lombardi code.

A man who belittles another—who is not charitable to another, who is not loyal, who speaks ill of another—is not a leader and does not belong in the top management echelon.

Coach Lombardi pointing the way.

MATURITY

Emotional maturity is a preface for a sense of values. The immature person exaggerates what is not important.

The mature person puts first things first. I do not mean he is a sad sack. He knows how to laugh and have fun. But he also knows what life is all about and what is expected of him as a reasonable human being.

A great sign of immaturity is to become very angry or hurt at the slightest criticism from others. A mature person profits from criticism.

MEETINGS

A meeting is only a means of communication. Its purpose should be to produce a change in procedure. This procedure could be in knowledge, attitude, behavior, or skill. In our meetings, management gives information, it collects information, it pools information, and it discusses the best way to approach the problem. We have one hard and fast rule: Once the group is agreed upon the method, there is no deviation until the group agrees to the change.

MISTAKES

You have to tread a careful line with mistakes. On the one hand, a team has to be ever-vigilant against mistakes, because any mistake—no matter how insignificant it may seem at the time—can cost you the game. On the other hand, you can't have players who are simply playing to avoid making a mistake. They must be conscious of mistakes but not paralyzed by the possibility of making one.

I think a lot of this has to do with a team's confidence in its level of preparation for a game both individually and as a team. If each player knows that the guys on either side of him will do their job, it helps him relax. The players don't have to do anything more than what's expected of them. Stated another way, if every player is doing his job, you don't need heroics to win. I think that my father knew this instinctively, and this knowledge was the basis for how he prepared his teams. Fundamentals and simplicity were the staples of his philosophy. With these, mistakes could be kept to a minimum.

A lot of this is developed over time. Every player is prepared physically and prepared mentally. They have confidence in the system and in the game plan. And they have confidence that the guys on either side of them will do their jobs. They know that they're not trying to win the game on their own. What this allows a player to do is play with poise, even under the most difficult circumstances.

A lot of quarterbacks feel they have to make the big play to win the game. When you're down on the twenty-yard line with four minutes left in the game and you're down by five points, you might—particularly a quarterback—be tempted to try to win the game with one play. But my father emphasized over and over to the Packers that if each player just did his job, they could play mistake-free football and ultimately win the game. This gave the players a sense of freedom, through discipline and repetition, and it allowed them to relax and play the game with poise.

A winning football team must avoid mistakes with a passion. Treat mistakes with a vengeance.

Constantly criticizing yourself for past mistakes and errors tends to precipitate the very thing you would like to avoid and change.

Hell, I can't just sit around and see an error being made and not say anything about it. I like to think I've had some experience in this business, and you don't win when you're making lots of errors. Nobody wants to be told he's making errors, not the way I tell them. But they've got to be told and told until they get to the point where they don't make them anymore.

MOTIVATION

Bart Starr to Lombardi: The shoutings, encouragements, inspirational messages, and vindictive assault on mistakes transcended the walls of our dressing rooms, but in the privacy of those same rooms to have known the bigger man—kneeling in tearful prayer

with his players after both triumph and defeat—was a strengthening experience that only your squads can ever fully appreciate.

Jim Taylor on Lombardi: It's the motivation that's the thing, and he knew just the right words, just the right approach to me. He knew how to handle me just like a parent handles his children to get the maximum out of them. Just the right approach to get me to listen, that was it. And he motivated me to the maximum. I don't think I could have given more.

My father made an opening day speech to Green Bay veterans on July 23, 1959, in which he set a baseline. He basically told the veterans from a 1-10-1 team to get serious or get out. "I'm going to find thirty-six men who have the pride to make any sacrifice to win. There are such men. If they're not here, I'll get them. I you are not one, if you don't want to play, you might as well leave right now."

It was a risk: The players weren't used to hearing this from anyone, and they didn't yet know who Vince Lombardi was. But nobody left, and from then on my father had them where he wanted them. This was his motivational gift: He seemed to have an instinct for just how far he could push people, how to make them angry and turn that anger into a burning desire to win.

Part of his gift was making his players want to prove to him how much they did want to win. After losing a key game to the Rams in 1965, my dad exploded at players before a practice, chewing them out in no uncertain terms and raging at them for not caring about winning.

Dammit, you guys don't care if you win or lose. I'm the only one that cares. I'm the only one that puts his blood and guts and his heart into the game! You guys show up, you listen a little bit, you concentrate . . . you've got the concentration of three-year-olds. You're nothing! I'm the only guy that gives a damn if we win or lose.

The reaction was just as explosive. The players fell over each other in their eagerness to prove just how much they did want to win. Forrest Gregg and Bob Skoronski, the Packers' offensive tackles, were ready to knock my dad down in their frustration and demanded to know how he could dare say that they lacked desire.

The reaction was just what my father wanted. In a few moments he was completely calm. "That's the kind of attitude I want! Who else feels that way?" Needless to say, everyone did. The whole team was united in a desire to prove to my father that they cared about winning as much as he did.

At other times his motivation could be of a kinder, gentler type. Once, before a crucial 1961 game against the Giants, he took the nervous Bart Starr aside and said, "I don't want you to do anything else today except what you've been doing all year. And I know you can do it."

He was also careful to pick the right words after a game. After a valiant effort in the 1960 title game that the Packers lost to Philadelphia, my father was more gentle than usual in his postgame comments: "Perhaps you didn't realize you could have won this game. But I think there's no doubt in your minds now. And that's why you will win it all next year. This will never happen again. You will never lose another championship."

There is a time when violent reactions are in order. And there are times when purring like a pussycat and bestowing thanks and gratitude are equally desirable. Each of us must learn when the time fits the response and must tailor our action or reaction to each situation.

My father said a number of times, "If I yell at you, five minutes later I don't know what I said and I don't know who I said it to." And I think to some degree that was true. But I also think that a lot of times he'd get on you and realize, "Oops, I went a little too far there. I'll have to find an opportunity to balance things out." And I also think part of it was that chewing someone out was a great way to motivate certain people.

Sometimes he would break a player down to rock bottom by design. And then an hour later or the next day he'd start the rebuilding process with a pat on the butt. For certain people this type of motivation elicited a tremendous response.

Two things were going on. I think my dad was as real as anybody could be in that kind of a situation. By the same token, he was calculating. You have to be. Not in a dishonest way, just, "How do I get the best out of this person? This player thinks he's giving me 100 percent, and I know he's only giving me 90. How do I get the extra 10?" You don't manipulate him, but you approach him, and push him, and pull him in a calculated manner.

There were some guys he knew he couldn't criticize because they couldn't handle it. He once said of Dan Currie, a Green Bay linebacker, "Criticism cuts so deep into Currie that I have to be careful. My first year here I read him out in front of the others just once, and I knew immediately that he resented it and that it wouldn't help. Even in private you have to be careful how you handle him, but if you tell him he's playing well, he'll go out there and kill himself for you." If criticism didn't work, he would always find another way.

I want you to be yourself. Just be what you are.

My father said these words to Sonny Jurgenson, the very talented Redskin quarterback. Talk about tailoring his message! Sonny's response, as he recalled it, was that he felt like running through a wall, anything just to let my father know that Sonny would do whatever he wanted.

Sonny was a player not unlike Paul Hornung. He had a reputation for appreciating the nightlife, and to some degree he did. My dad was not a Boy Scout, and he didn't expect his players to be Boy Scouts. He had rules that he knew some people were going to break. But when you really got down to it, if you were on time, if you gave him an effort in practice and then gave him a real effort in a game, he was capable of looking the other way.

On the other hand, he didn't want you getting in serious trouble or getting the attention of the media. He was very cognizant of the public perception of his team. If a player was out carousing and started people talking in a way that would reflect poorly on the team, my father had no patience with that.

This is not easy, this effort, day after day, week after week, to keep them up, but it is essential. Each week there is a different challenge, but there is also that unavoidable degree of sameness to these meetings.

I'm just going to give these guys complete hell today. . . . Today is going to be one of those days.

In the good old days motivation was simple. You got rid of the guys who weren't motivated. I think it's tougher today. Today you have to worry about striking the balance between "we're going to do it my way" and creating buy-in—having it be their idea.

Back when my father coached, guys weren't making much money. Fifty grand was a big salary. In the late 1960s, when the AFL came along, some players were starting to make good money, but the money still wasn't there in terms of players making more than coaches. To a great extent the players still said, "Well, if the coach says so, I guess I'm going to do it."

Plus, you had a lot of people, at least by their own accounts, who felt it was either football or the coal mines. It was taking orders from the coach or driving a truck for the local park program. Today you still have a little bit of that, but the players are making so much money that telling them "Do it my way" without explaining the reason why doesn't work nearly as well.

When you are flat, you're always looking for that big play or that big man who will bring you out of it.

Sometimes it will be the opponents who suddenly, and by something they do, pick your club up. One of their players will swing at one of yours, or they will pile on. On the sideline, because you have been trying everything you know but with no success, you have been praying for something like this, and now it's a different ball game.

The player must be determined that every one of those spectators will leave the stadium after the game convinced they have seen the best halfback in the country.

Anybody who is a leader, who spends every day trying to motivate people, eventually is going to run out of things to say. That's why coaches and managers move around so much. You need a new audience, a new challenge. After nine seasons with the Packers, what could my father tell his players—some of whom had been with him the whole nine years—that was new and different? They had already won the championship five times. What could motivate them to make that supreme effort yet again? I don't think he left Green Bay because he feared the inevitable decline of the Packers so much as he thought to himself, "What more can I say? What more can I do? And if I can't get them motivated to play their best, I'm letting both them and myself down."

*Jousting with the press, one of Coach Lombardi's
least favorite duties.*

NEW JOB

The most difficult part of a new job is analyzing and understanding the personality of each player.

It is unwise to walk into a new job with a complete new staff.

The two main things on a new job are the personality analysis and a talent analysis. The idea is to make sure that every player is in his best position.

This is sound advice not only for a new coach but for anyone taking on a new leadership position. You've probably been hired because things are not going too well, but it would be a mistake to assume that there aren't capable people on hand who just need some direction. Making immediate wholesale changes will demoralize your entire department. That being said, after a thorough analysis of your situation, you may have to clean house if for no other reason than to send a message to everyone.

NUNS

Watch Dress in Halls and Dining Hall— *Nuns.*

During training camp the Packers stayed at Saint Norbert College, a Catholic institution that had a lot of nuns on campus for summer school. My father had a deep respect for the commitment and sacrifice those nuns made in serving in a religious order. The words above are notes to himself from a speech that he gave in training camp.

Paul Hornung roasting Coach Lombardi,
who seems to be enjoying it.

OPPONENTS

We do love our opponent in that we have respect for his ability and for his dignity as a man. There's also a hate for your competition in that he is your competitor and he is the one that is actually preventing you from winning.

In my business, we believe in knowing everything we possibly can about the competition. Every player on the team makes out a complete report on his opponent. We want to know all the characteristics of the man on the other team. The pluses and minuses you might want to call it. Another way of putting it is a man-to-man analysis. . . . We consider that vital. We even go further than that. We put all this information into a computer. So the next time we play them, we know all there is to know about the opponent.

You never lose a game if your opponent doesn't score.

*Coach Lombardi preached being in good physical condition;
once in a while he practiced what he preached.*

PAIN

In my father's opinion, pain was part of the equation in football, as it was in life. He had little patience for players with a low tolerance for pain, for those who would nurse small hurts and let them interfere with the task at hand. His players used to say that *their* pain never bothered him.

When he walked into the Packers' trainer's room on the morning after the first full day of workouts during his first season with the squad, he was disgusted with the number of players he found there. "There must have been fifteen or twenty of them waiting for the whirlpool bath or the diathermy or for rubdowns," he complained. "What is this, an emergency casualty ward?" he bellowed. "Now get this straight. When you're hurt, you'll get the best medical attention we can provide. We've got too much money invested in you to think otherwise, but this has got to stop. This is disgraceful. I have no patience for the small hurts that are bothering most of you."

Honesty makes me add, however, that my dad was not the most stoic sufferer I've ever known. During his own football career he was more often than not sidelined with injuries. And when he was in pain later in life, you can bet we heard about it. I remember once "sharing" with him a late-night drive home to Green Bay from Milwaukee. It was a question of staying in Milwaukee overnight or driving home. He was the one who wanted to drive home, and he persuaded me that if we split the driving, it wouldn't be too difficult. After about five minutes, however, he started to complain about his knee . . . and I drove the entire way.

You're going to have to learn to live with small hurts and play with small hurts if you're going to play for me.

I have to first sell them on themselves and then on the small hurts, because the small hurts are not only a part of football but also a part of life.

Many hurts are a small price to pay for having won.

Jerry Kramer has the perfect devil-may-care attitude it takes to play this game. He not only ignores the small hurts but the large ones, too, and the evidence of his indifference is all over his body.

PATIENCE

If I had to do things all over again, I think I would pray for more patience maybe, and more understanding.

This is one of my favorite quotes. Sometimes, in overcoming our shortcomings, prayer is the only answer.

PATTERNS

All well-coached clubs have patterns.

This is true, but I might add that the poorer teams have patterns that the better teams use to defeat them.

PERFECTION

Being a perfectionist is what made my father who he was, and therefore it was something everyone around him had to put up with. If you demand excellence, as my father did, perfectionism is something that you—and those around you—have to live with. It's much easier to let things slide, to take the path of least resistance. Perfectionism rocks the boat. It upsets some people. It will lead to some conflicts on a team, and it translates into hard work for everyone. If a leader slacks off, looks the other way, and allows excuses, it's a lot easier. Easier perhaps, but you will lose. But that was never my father's way. He strove for perfection twenty-four hours a day, seven days a week, and he pushed everyone around him to do the same.

If your commitment to perfection is only part-time, it doesn't matter how intense you are. It's not hard to be a perfectionist four days out of five, but to demand perfection every day, every minute, from everybody—that's tough. But it's the only way to succeed.

No one is perfect. But boys, if you'll not settle for anything less than the best, you will be amazed at what you can do with your lives. You will be amazed at how much you can rise in this world.

The satisfactions are few, I guess, for perfectionists, but I have never known a good coach who wasn't one.

The closer you get to the goal line, the more perfect you should be.

If Max [McGee] were a perfectionist, there's no telling how great a receiver he might be, but then, pressing all the time as perfectionists must, he would probably lose one of his greatest assets, his ability to relax. He can relax before, during, and after a game, and it makes him a great clutch player, although it also contributes to his tendency to be a little careless.

PERSISTENCE

I know of no way but to persist.

PLAYS

I realized that in pro ball it is to our advantage not to run to a specific hole but to run to daylight. We started to coach it, and that was the beginning of that.

POTENTIAL

A guy may have the potential to be the best player of all time. He's able, agile, and intelligent. Yet unless he is totally committed to the team and victory as a unit, he won't win ball games. And winning is the name of the game.

It's only asking a man to live up to his potential. If you don't, you cheat. You cheat on yourself and your company.

POWER

We cannot allow the innocent among us to be beguiled by the few who seek power through destruction.

PREJUDICE

As an Italian-American raised in the Northeast in the early twentieth century, my father experienced prejudice. Once you experience it, you will not tolerate it in those around you.

If you're black or white, you're a part of the family. We make no issue over a man's color.

I just won't tolerate anybody in this organization, coach or player, making it an issue. We respect every man's dignity, black or white. I won't stand for any movements or groups on our ball club. It comes down to a question of love. . . . You just have to love your fellow man, and it doesn't matter whether he is black or white. If anything is bothering any of our players—black and white alike—we settle whatever it is right away.

If I ever hear nigger or dago or kike or anything like that around here, regardless of who you are, you're through with me. You can't play for me if you have any kind of prejudice.

I can tell you how many players I have on the squad, and I can tell you which ones aren't going to be here next year. But I can't tell you how many are black and how many are white.

PREPARATION

The type of preparation evinced by the quotes here is routine in the NFL today. In the late 1950s and 1960s it was unique.

The option play was one of the first things I put in when I left West Point for the Giants in 1954 and after I had spent that whole winter looking at the Giants' movies. It was in that brick split-level we had just moved into in Oradell, New Jersey, and I put up the screen in the den. I ran that projector back and forth, night and day, until it began to drive Marie and the kids crazy, and I had to take it down to the basement.

I was trying, never having played pro ball and having seen very little of it, to get a full picture of what not only the Giants but everybody in the league was doing, and so I'd chart every play and every defense. On each play in every game, I'd run the projector back and forth three or four times with seven or eight people in mind, and then I'd run it back again to see what the three or four others were doing. I filled up those yellow legal pads, and then I indexed the pads.

For every hour of game play that we put in at that stadium and at the others around the league, we put in fourteen on those [practice] fields. That is preseason and during the season, and then there are those equal hours spent in those meetings, and all of this does not include the time we coaches spend in preparation for those practice sessions and those meetings, and that time seems to me to be almost incalculable.

From morning until night and week after week in those first months here in 1959, we ran and reran the films of the eighteen previous Packer games. We graded every player, and then each coach sat down and wrote a report on each, and we compared these and came to our conclusions.

We keep an open file—a running record—of every ballplayer in the league, and during the off-season we regrade every player off our own films and off the films we can get of the teams we haven't played.

PRESSURE

The most important thing a coach needs is the knowledge that his team can or can't play under pressure. If it can't, you need new players; if it can, you can make do with average ones.

We may have as many as thirty-five rookies report to camp. Only five or six will be there at the end. And I have about four weeks to make my decision as to whether it's go or no-go. If he doesn't have the ability or talent, it's easy. Yet when he obviously has ability, talent, and agility, everything about him looks good, I still have to figure out how he will react with 60,000 people screaming in his ear.

We put tremendous pressure on the rookie in training camp. Purposely. There's pressure on the veterans, too, after a six-month holiday, but at least you already know their strengths and weaknesses. Some of them put on a little weight and perhaps get a little lazy. We know how to correct that.

Team not responding, offensively or defensively. Not reacting to pressure. My job to increase that pressure.

These words are taken from my father's notes to the Redskin squad on July 21, 1969. It's a deceptively simple statement that goes to the heart of his leadership philosophy. Pressure and stress are a constant today in every walk of life, and a team that doesn't—or can't—respond appropriately to pressure will not succeed. Therefore, a leader's job is to increase the pressure until his or her people begin to respond appropriately. My father never saw his job as simply helping a team come up with a set of plays that would best counter another team's set of plays. His role was to take those men beyond themselves and bring forth from them more than they thought was possible. He wanted his Packer and Redskin teams to be like a finely honed machine responding to the lightest touch of the controls. When they didn't respond, it was his job to turn up the heat.

The pressure of losing is bad, awful, because it kills you eventually. But the pressure of winning is worse, infinitely worse, because it keeps on torturing you and torturing you and torturing you. At Green Bay I was winning one championship after another, after another, after another. I couldn't take it, because I blamed myself, damned myself, whenever they lost a game. I couldn't ever forgive myself for a loss, because I felt I'd let them down. I felt I wouldn't be able to raise

myself to the right pitch for the big games, and then I wouldn't be able to raise them to their best effort.

In a nutshell, this is why he stepped down from coaching after the 1967 season.

PRIDE

Pride is a tricky concept. In many quarters it has acquired a bad reputation. Too often, ego and confidence taken to an extreme is mistakenly labeled pride. This is not pride, it's hubris. Hubris is the belief that you know better than anyone else, and it has caused the downfall of many people. Pride, on the other hand, is that determination—fierce at times—to never do less than your best. After all, as my father said, your name is on the effort.

The trouble with me is that my ego just can't accept a loss. If I were more perfectly adjusted, I could toss off defeat, but my name is on this ball club. Thirty-six men publicly reflect me and reflect on me, and it's a matter of my pride.

Pride is developed by a winning tradition and a winning history. You must have pride

to win consistently, and you must win consistently to establish a winning tradition that
sustains and develops pride.

When two teams meet that are equal in ability and execution, it's the team that has
pride that wins.

PRINCIPLES

If a man who is considered a leader is to stay
a leader, he must be prepared to adhere to
his principles if he is certain, in his own con-
science, that he is doing right.

You don't do what is right once in a while,
but all of the time.

Morally, the life of the organization must be
of exemplary nature. This is one phase where
the organization must not have criticism.

Each of us must be prepared to adhere to his
principles, if he is certain in his own con-
science that he is doing right, if he is getting
the job done to his satisfaction and to the
approbation of the various publics he serves.

PROTESTERS

You hear the expression that this is the "now generation," but I don't think that's quite the right interpretation. I would call it the *why* generation. They don't want a yes or no. They're asking why. We can't have them defying authority on such places as campuses, but that's not the whole story. They're raising some questions that aren't being answered.

We've got the young radicals who are throwing bombs at property, and we've got radicals on the other side who don't want anybody to talk. Neither of them is worth a damn.

PUNCTUALITY

I believe a man should be on time—not a minute late, not 10 seconds late—but on time for things. I believe that a man who's late for meetings or for the bus won't run his pass routes right. He'll be sloppy.

PUNTING

When in doubt, punt.

PURPOSE

I'm not better or less than the next man. But the thing about me is that I always knew what my acts would mean. I was lucky. I fell into football, really. I had some early successes at coaching in high school. . . . I knew then, as a young man, the path I had to follow. Now, the earlier in life you know your track, the better off you are. I was lucky and found a singleness of purpose early on.

The man who succeeds above his fellow man is the one who early in life clearly discerns his objective, and toward that objective he directs all of his powers.

PURSUIT

Pursuit is an all out effort on defense—a spurt to a collision.

Watching an end zone play with
backup quarterback Zeke Bratkowski.

QUITTING

Once you learn to quit, it becomes a habit.

The harder you work, the harder it is to surrender.

If you quit now, during these workouts, you'll quit in the middle of the season in a game. Once you learn to quit, it becomes a habit. We don't want anyone here who'll quit. We want 100 percent out of every individual, and if you don't want to give it, get out. Just get up and get out right now.

QUARTERBACKS

I believe you can confuse the QB with too many don'ts.

There are four attributes to a QB:
1. The ability to think under pressure
2. The ability to transmit commonsense knowledge to teammates
3. A quality of leadership
4. A talent for thinking through things and the ability to reason instead of reckless gambling

Of all the people on your ball club—and you are involved with all of them—there is no other with whom you spend as much time as you do with your quarterback. If this is a game through which you find self-expression—and if it isn't, you don't belong in it—then that quarterback is the primary extension of yourself and is your greatest challenge.

The mark of a great quarterback is the ability to stay away from stupid calls. The gambling QB disappears fast.

A quarterback must have sure hands and be an excellent passer. His IQ must be above average, because he must not only be able to absorb the coach's game plan each week, he must also have a thorough knowledge of what everyone does on every play, and he must know the opponent, the qualities and characteristics of each individual on the other team. He should be strong physically and able to take punishment, and he should have enough height to see his receivers over those opposing linemen. A quarterback must have great poise, too, and he must not be panicked by what the defense does or what his own offense fails to do. He must know the characteristic fakes and patterns of his ends and backs and anticipate the break before the receiver makes it. If you find all this in one man, you have found a special person.

Deep in thought.

REGRETS

Leave no regrets on the field.

RELAXING

Lombardi on Don Hutson, Packer Hall of Fame receiver and cohost on WBAY's *The Vince Lombardi Show*: He has the ability to relax that all great receivers, or performers, must have.

Bart's too tense, I'm thinking. . . . Bart feels that he has the whole burden of our offense on his shoulders, and I will have to try to relax him.

My father relaxed very little. As soon as one game was over, he would start stewing about the next one. For my father, relaxation during the season was a couple of drinks over dinner with friends late in the week. During the off-season, golf—which actually wasn't all that relaxing the way my father played it—was just an intense focus on something other than football.

He realized, however, that it was important for the players to be able to relax once in a while. Getting them up for a game was a complicated matter of excitement without too much tension. For the big games this was sometimes a difficult balance to achieve. Stepping onto the bus that would take the Packers to the first "Super Bowl" game against the Kansas City Chiefs, my dad stopped the driver for a minute to do a soft-shoe dance in the aisle. "They were too tight," he later explained.

REPETITION

George Halas on Lombardi: You might reduce Lombardi's coaching philosophy to a single sentence: In any game, you do the things you do best and you do them over and over and over.

You teach discipline by doing it over and over, by repetition and rote.

A player must be trained thoroughly. He must repeat the same drills over and over in practice so that he automatically responds to a situation.

My father's concept of "running to daylight" seems pretty simple at first glance. The running back just finds the hole where the defense is not—in other words, daylight. But you can't do this on your own. To make this possible, the blocker ahead of you must take his guy out of your way, and then you have to react off the block. There's no time in the middle of the play to think about what you're doing or to plan your next move. To fully understand running to daylight—and be successful at it—you have to drill it so many times that it becomes second nature. Repetition is the key—working the play into the ground of your subconscious until you literally don't have to think, you just do it.

In this game you must repeat everything often enough to reach the slowest member of your team, because a single mistake can ruin the work of ten others. The problem is to keep from boring some of those others.

RESPECT

You show me a man who belittles another and I will show you a man who is not a leader or one who is not charitable, who has no respect for the dignity of another, is not loyal, and I will show you a man who is not a leader.

If a leader is sensitive to the emotional needs and expectations of others, the attitude toward the leader from the group will be one of confidence fused with affection.

RISKS

All your effort in any business should be directed to taking the risks out of it. If you don't believe that, give up on what you're doing and play the horses.

All the world loves a loser, but they are simply nuts about a gambler.

RUNNING GAME

1. Know strongest blockers.
2. Run at tired or dazed defenders.

3. **Run at weak links on plays of importance.**

4. **Don't depend on making ten yards consistently.**

5. **The best play is always the best call on first down—get as much yardage.**

6. **Second and short—still best possible situation.**

7. **Stick to running game if good; don't switch for the sake of switching.**

8. **Inside and outside.**

9. **Don't be patterned according to down or position.**

These are from notes that my father made to himself, and the shorthand isn't always completely clear. But it sketches out his approach in an interesting way.

*Coach Lombardi pointing out something
he thinks the referee missed.*

SACRIFICE

Sacrifice was a concept drilled into my dad by his father and later by his seminary training. He often talked of paying the price, as in "To accomplish anything worthwhile, you must pay the price." In other words, sacrifice. It's an idea that some younger readers may find unique. We don't hear much about sacrifice these days. That's unfortunate. To achieve a goal, you must be willing to pay a price.

Another post to aim at is the spirit of self-sacrifice. If we are to improve and reach a certain degree of perfection, we must make sacrifices. Once you have made up your mind that you are going to reach a certain goal, you must train yourself to qualify for it.

Every vocation calls for sacrifices of time, energy, mind, and body.

A man can be as great as he wants to be. If you believe in yourself and have the courage, the determination, the dedication, the competitive drive, and if you are willing to sacrifice the little things in life and pay the price for the things that are worthwhile, it can be done.

When I speak of "Spartanism," I'm speaking not so much of leaving the weak to die, but I'm speaking of the Spartan quality of sacrifice, and the Spartan quality of self-denial.

SECOND PLACE

Second place is meaningless. You can't always be first, but you have to believe that you should have been—that you are never beaten, time just runs out on you.

SELF-EXPRESSION

Everybody chooses to put his own signature on things. My father certainly had his own methods, and he wouldn't have been comfortable trying to use some other coach's plays or system. The head coach of the Giants when my dad was an assistant, Jim Lee Howell, sometimes said that he was there only to make sure the footballs were inflated correctly. That was his way. But that style never would have worked for my father.

Simply put, the team had to conform to my father's ideals and self-expression. He did learn through experience that there were limits, however. He couldn't force people to be something they weren't. Take Herb Adderley, for example, Green Bay's first draft pick in 1961. Adderley had lots of speed and open-field running ability. My father wanted to use him as an offensive back, but there was a lot of talent at that position already. Instead, according to my father, "I tried to make a flanker out of him. I was going to use his speed, and on the practice field when we found out he had good hands and was real natural running those pass routes, we thought we had it made. Then we put him in a game, and nothing happened." As it turned out, Adderley really wanted to be a defensive back. "For a whole half season I had been so stubborn that I had been trying the impossible." Good thing, too: Adderley went on to become an all-pro cornerback.

A team expresses a coach's personality and its own personality, and this doesn't change from week to week.

I've seen coaches who, seeing that someone had success with something, immediately tried to take it for themselves. It didn't work because it didn't fit them. It didn't express their personalities.

In all my years of coaching, I have never been successful using somebody else's play.

The successful man is himself.

When you start to coach, you coach the system you played, but you begin almost immediately to discard what doesn't fit you or your material, and you look for what does. . . . All of us are takers, but if a person can't add something to what he takes from others, he should get out.

SIMPLICITY

Almost always, the plan is too complex. Too much to learn and perfect in too little time.

Quoting General Douglas MacArthur: Simplicity is the sign of true greatness, and meekness is the sign of true strength.

Simplicity is a form of humility, and simplicity is a sign of true greatness. Meekness is a sign of humility, and meekness is a sign of true strength.

General Douglas MacArthur was one of my father's idols. MacArthur was, of course, a graduate of West Point and was the commandant up there for a while. He was very close to Red Blaik, my father's head coach when he worked at Army. MacArthur was a great fan of Army football; in fact, during the World War II the first thing MacArthur wanted to know on a Sunday morning was how the Army team had done the day before.

When MacArthur retired, one of my father's regular tasks was taking film of the Army games to MacArthur's suite in the Waldorf-Astoria Hotel and giving the general a play-by-play analysis of the game. The two would talk football and more, and these conversations had an immense influence on my father. Much of his philosophy of coaching—and winning—can be traced back to the general.

My dad would often play MacArthur's famous speech to the West Point cadets in the coach's dressing room: "Old soldiers never die, they just fade away. . . . The corps, the corps, the corps." It's a great speech. He played it frequently and would often tear up when he heard it.

My father's approach to football was quite simple. His playbook was smaller than those of most other coaches, and he asked his players to remember less than other coaches did. Simplicity—combined with discipline—was a hallmark of his method. He often said that the perfect name for the perfect football coach would be "Simple Simon Legree." This was a tongue-in-cheek comment, of course, but he liked the combination of simplicity and slave driving implied in this fusion of personalities.

One word of caution—keep attack simple.

If you can hit the other people where they're strongest and break them there, it's all over.

If you can bring down their best men, it's all over.

You are foolish if you don't go at a team's weaknesses.

I never said my father was consistent!

STRENGTHS, PLAYING TO YOUR

What it will all come down to again on Sunday, I'm thinking, is that we will both try

to do what we do best. We know everything they can do, and they know everything we can do, so we will both go with our strengths.

The element of surprise may have temporary value . . . but both of us can be reasonably sure that the other team is not really going to change because only a grossly inferior team should ever depart or deviate from its strength to win. Even surprise should be based on deception and rapidity of maneuver and not radical change.

SUCCESS

Success is not a sometime thing—it is an all-time thing.

I don't know of anything that really qualifies me as an absolute authority on success or failure.

To be successful, you've got to be honest with yourself.

Success rests not only on ability, but upon commitment, loyalty, and pride.

Success in anything in this world is 75 percent mental. In our league, most times the teams are evenly matched in ability and physically. And it is usually the team that is best mentally prepared on that particular day which wins the ballgame.

Finding new talent is the lifeblood of a successful football team.

Success is paying the price. You have got to pay the price to win—to get there and to stay there. Success is not a sometime thing; it is an all the time thing. You don't do what is right once in awhile, but all of the time—success is a habit, winning is a habit. Unfortunately, so is losing.

Once you agree upon the price you and your family must pay for success, it enables you to ignore the minor hurts, the opponent's pressure, and temporary failures.

What success does to you. It is like a habit-forming drug that in victory saps your elation and in defeat deepens your despair. Once you have sampled it, you are hooked.

**I think you realize now that success is much
more difficult to live with than failure. I don't
think anyone realizes, except ourselves, the
obstacles we had to face week after week.**

This quote is from an early 1963 letter to the Packers
after a dramatic defeat of the Giants in Yankee
Stadium in the 1962 championship game. Nobody
knew better than my father just how difficult success
was. The more he won, the more pressure he felt to
keep on winning.

Sweep, The Packer

Before it was the Packer sweep, it was the Giants sweep,
and before that it was the Los Angeles Rams sweep. My
father first taught this very successful play to the Giants
in the summer of 1954 after hours of watching and analyzing film of the Rams.

The sweep was such a successful play that as
an opponent you would practice to stop it and would
always be anticipating it. The moment you sensed it coming, you reacted to it. But in stopping it you opened
yourself up to a play that looked like the sweep but would
hit a different hole. The success of one play sets up the
success of another.

There's nothing spectacular about it. It's just a yard gainer, and I've diagrammed it so many times and coached it so much and watched it evolve so often since I first put it in with the Giants eight years ago that I think I see it in my sleep.

Behind all that is the basic truth that it expresses you as a coach and the players as a team, and they feel good when they execute it and it's completely right.

A play's value is not only in that play itself but in the counter it sets up.

*Paul Hornung joked that in this picture
Coach Lombardi was hearing his confession.*

TEACHING

They call it coaching, but it is teaching. You do not just tell them it is so, but you show them reasons why it is so, and you repeat and repeat until they are convinced, until they know.

I believe I wanted to be a teacher more than a coach.

We concentrate on the "whys." I never tell a player, "This is my way, now do it." Instead, I say, "This is the way we do it, and this is why we do it."

That first year [at Saint Cecilia's], before I got my courses set, it was like it is every year

in this game. In each course it was a case of keeping one lesson ahead of the class, which is what we have to do here, week after week and game after game.

When my father took his first job at Saint Cecilia's High School, he perceived his job first and foremost as a teacher, not as a football coach. That's where he thought he was headed. Slowly, the football just took over.

But he continued to act on the belief that a large part of coaching was being a teacher. I think he liked that part. I think he knew that when he was up in front of the team, his teaching ability was critical. A lot of coaches who have been in the business for a long time don't have a command of the teaching aspects of the job. He excelled at it, and his players always recognized that and responded to it.

Bart Starr on Lombardi: He left no doubt what he expected, and—more important— explained why.

Sonny Jurgensen on Lombardi: Everything has a reason, a meaning. It makes it much easier to play the game.

TEAM

The importance of the team concept to my father can't be underestimated. From the matching green sport coats that the team wore to away games to the ritual Thanksgiving dinners with the whole team and their families, everything was calculated to get each individual to think of himself as part of the larger unit. Each individual had to play his best, but it didn't stop there: Each individual also needed to know that his success depended on his teammates playing their best too, and if you didn't play your best, you were letting your teammates down.

On the field, eleven guys have to make it with each other—as a single unit. I know of no other game where interdependence of teammates is more critical. Each has to make a personal commitment to excellence, really to victory—as a single unit. That's why we have coaches. It is their responsibility to create a "coordinated efficiency" out of eleven hard-driving, eager, highly individual athletes.

You fit your game to the talents and personality of your team, as well as to your own.

"Selflessness," as opposed to "selfishness," is what I try to teach. "Do your damnedest. Give everything you've got, because you are playing with the greatest group, the greatest team, yet to swing out onto a battlefield." If you can instill that, you can win ball games.

The only true satisfaction a player receives is the satisfaction that comes from being part of a successful team.

Build for your team a feeling of oneness, of dependence upon one another, and of strength to be derived from unity.

Each man must contribute to the spirit, and this spirit is the cohesive force that binds eleven hardened and talented men into an irresistible force.

The second characteristic of a mature person is what is called a sense of responsibility. We must place the demands of duty above our own comfort. We are part of a team—in the family, at school, in games, in work—and we must contribute our share to the team effort.

In my field we bring every man to think in terms of team effort. We develop a cohesive machine in which the color lines disappear and the various national origins are nonexistent.

The team transcended the highly fraught issue of race for my father. After experiencing the fragmentation of separate accommodations in the South during a 1960 preseason game, my father decided never to allow the team to be housed separately again. Hotels would take all or none of the Packers. Furthermore, my father made it clear to the tavern and restaurant owners in Green Bay that any establishment that didn't welcome the entire team would not be patronized by anyone on the team.

Bart Starr on Lombardi: Lombardi explained that some of the players on the team were going to be famous, some obscure, but everyone was equally important. For us to succeed, we had to place our personal goals behind those of the team. We had to pick each other up and push each other to higher levels.

TOUGHNESS, MENTAL

When they ask me what [mental toughness] is, I have difficulty explaining it. I think it is singleness of purpose, and once you have agreed upon the price that you and your family must pay for success, it enables you to forget that price. It enables you to ignore the minor hurts, the opponent's pressure, and the temporary failures.

Mental toughness was a favorite theme for my father. He talked about it constantly and plastered the locker room with signs about the importance of mental toughness, such as "Physical toughness will make the opponent weaken, and mental toughness will make him crack." In a letter that my father wrote to his players after the 1962 championship game, he told them, "The Giants tried to intimidate us physically, but in the final analysis we were mentally tougher than they were, and that same mental toughness made them crack." Another of his favorite statements about mental toughness was honed and refined over the years, finally culminating in this often-quoted phrase from his last speech as coach of the Green Bay Packers: "Mental toughness is the perfectly disciplined will—and the will, gentlemen, is the character in action." Other variations on the theme are found below.

The most important element in the character makeup is mental toughness.

Mental toughness is humility. Mental toughness is a disciplined will above anything else. What I mean by that is that disciplined will is your own character in action.

Mental toughness is many things and is rather difficult to explain. Its qualities are sacrifice and self-denial. Also, most importantly, it is combined with the perfectly disciplined will, which refuses to give in. It's a state of mind—you could call it "character in action."

Over the years, for better or for worse, I have picked up a reputation for being tough. I admit I have mixed emotions about that reputation, particularly when one of my former players was asked what it was like to work for me. His answer was, "Well, I will tell you what it is like in a nutshell: When Lombardi turns to us in the locker room and tells us to sit down, I don't even look for a chair."

If football did not demand sternness and toughness, everyone would be a champion.

There are occasions when being hard and tough immediately is the easiest and kindest way in the long run. We have to be hard sometimes to get the most out of our people, out of ourselves, and what sometimes can appear to be a cruel move at the moment can turn out to be a blessing in the long run for the man, for yourself, and for your organization.

My father demanded mental toughness from everyone around him (his family included). He seemed to know just how hard he could push people in order to get the results he wanted. In the long run many of his players were grateful for what his demanding toughness brought out in them . . . even if the process was rarely painless!

I can't put my finger on just what I learned playing . . . in those scoreless games, but it was something. A certain toughness.

Some of his legendary toughness came from my father's own football experiences. In later years he would remember his Fordham career with a special fondness. Some of the games were brutal, low-scoring defensive duels in which stamina became paramount and the will to win became more important than talent or strategy. It was in these early contests as a player that my father found his true strengths on the field. He was not a great player, but his determination made up for the skills he lacked.

Dear Tim: If you want to make Saint Bede's football team, you must be mentally tough. Best, Vince Lombardi.

This is from a letter that Art Rooney, the patriarch of the Pittsburgh Steelers, asked my father to write to a ten-year-old who was trying out for his school's team.

*Coach Lombardi drilling his players
in the fundamentals.*

Victory

The ultimate victory must be pursued and wooed with all of one's might.

To be successful in life demands that each man make a personal commitment to excellence and to victory, even though we know deep down that the ultimate victory can never be completely won. Yet that victory must be pursued, and it must be wooed with every fiber of our body, with every bit of our might, and with all our effort.

There was glory in my father's concept of football. A game was not just a game—it was also a battle, a crusade, the ultimate test of a man. Often his discussions of the game reflected the epic struggle of good versus evil. This conviction, though it made him difficult to live with at times, led directly to his success. It made him not only struggle against all odds to win but also welcome those odds as the sweetest element of his ultimate success.

I believe that man's greatest hour, his finest fulfillment, is that moment when he has worked his heart out in a good cause and lies exhausted on the field of battle—exhausted but victorious.

The value of all our daily efforts is greater and more enduring if they create in each one of us a person who grows and understands and really lives. Or one who prevails for a larger and more meaningful victory—not only now but in time and, hopefully, in eternity.

VISION

The difference is knowing what you want, knowing what the end is supposed to look like. If a coach doesn't know what the end is supposed to look like, he won't know it when he sees it.

Of course, this is accepted management wisdom today, but it was pretty much cutting-edge in the 1960s.

*Coach Lombardi was focused and driven
but at times he also felt fatigue.*

WEATHER

You've got to be bigger than the weather to win.

My father said this to his team before the famous "Ice Bowl," the 1967 NFL championship game against the Dallas Cowboys. The Packers took his words to heart; they were bigger than the subzero temperature, and they won.

WILL

One of my dad's favorite sayings was, "Character is the will in action." As David Maraniss points out in *When Pride Still Mattered*, these were the words of his Fordham tutors now being passed on to another generation of students, this time on the football field instead of in the classroom.

People do not lack strength, they lack will.

The championships, the money, the color; all of these things linger only in the memory. It is the spirit, the will to excel, the will to win; these are the things that endure.

A team's strength is in its will—will in character and action.

The difference between the group and its leader is not in the lack of strength, not in the lack of knowledge, but rather in the lack of will.

WINNING

My dad has often been credited with the phrase "Winning isn't everything, it's the only thing." Actually, this famous line can be traced back to UCLA football coach Red Sanders, but it did show up on the walls of the Packers' locker room at times, and for many, the phrase became inseparable from the persona of Vince Lombardi.

On many levels my dad believed this, but he also felt uncomfortable at times with some of the implications of the phrase. He worked his way through several modifications over the years, including, "Winning isn't everything, but trying to win is," and "Winning isn't everything, but it sure beats what comes second." The original, however, does capture some of the passion that my dad felt on the subject. As he saw it, every win was critical and every loss hurt.

Take my dad's response to the 1960 Packers season, for example. The team lost the title game in a heart-breakingly close contest with the Philadelphia Eagles after an otherwise successful season, but it wasn't their many wins that he wanted to talk about at the start of the next year's training camp. "Many would consider the 1960 season a very successful one," he railed. "But you and I both know there is no second place. In this league you either win or you are last."

He would do anything within his power—and the power of those under his command—to win, including pushing his players to perform beyond their own perceptions of their limits and demanding the utmost commitment from every member of the team. This is certainly not to say that he tolerated dishonest means of achieving a victory, a notion that appalled his Jesuit-derived (and West Point–nurtured) code of honor. He was known to pull players from games if they resorted to playing outside the rules. But all other tactics were fair in his coaching philosophy: inspiring his players, needling them, teasing them, at times even verbally abusing them.

There's no question that his relentless pushing in the name of victory led to the extraordinary success of his teams. However, it must be said that my father's demanding coaching style was dependent on that same success. In other words, my father couldn't have gotten away with his demanding, pushing style if his teams hadn't been successful. His players would not have put up with his demands if the results had not proved he was right. As my dad realized, if you lead a team to victory, they'll do anything you ask because everyone wants to win—partly for the feeling of winning but also because they find themselves part of something transcendent, something larger than themselves, something that they could never have accomplished on their own.

My dad recognized that what he asked wasn't easy, and he recognized the resentment it created. But he also knew that it was the only way to achieve excellence, to win, to get the results that were expected of him and his team. And ultimately, that was what mattered the most.

My father's pursuit of winning was partly a result of his personality: an intense focus and a competitive nature that found release only in victory. And partly it was his upbringing by a demanding father, his seminary training, and his football lineage: the combined influence of West Point coach Red Blaik and General Douglas MacArthur. Blaik's creed, summed up in a phrase taped to the walls of the Army dressing room, "There is a vast difference between a good sport and a good loser," resonated deeply with my dad. MacArthur was another strong influence, one of the few men my dad actually revered. MacArthur's often-quoted statement, "There is no substitute for victory," comes the closest to explaining my dad's hunger for winning, and it was a phrase that he repeated often.

Winning is not a sometime thing here. It is an all-the-time thing. You don't win once in a while, you don't do things right once in a while, you do them right all the time.

You don't have to win 'em aesthetically. You win 'em the best you can.

True enough, but this never stopped my dad from engaging in all the preparation he possibly could. He was famous for watching tapes of the games in every spare moment, analyzing and reanalyzing every move of both his own players and the opposing team.

I don't give a damn about statistics as long as we win.

You must forget about being cautious, because if you don't, you're licked before you start. There is nothing to be afraid of as

long as you are aggressive and keep going. Keep going and you will win.

There's not enough thought, not enough dedication to winning. There's too many outside interests, too much bow hunting, and all this other extracurricular whatnot.

These were my father's words to his team after a loss. His frustration is evident here; clearly, he felt that the team wasn't concentrating on what mattered, and without that concentration, they would never prevail.

How does one achieve success in battle? I believe it is essential to understand that battles are won primarily in the hearts of men. Men respond to leadership in a most remarkable way. Once you have won their hearts, they will follow you anywhere.

A guy may have the potential to be the best player of all time. He's able, agile, and intelligent. Yet unless he is totally committed to the team and victory as a unit, he won't win ball games. And winning is the name of the game.

Each of us, if we would grow, must be committed to excellence and to victory. Even

though we know complete victory cannot be attained, it must be pursued with all one's might.

My dad believed that determination conquers all odds. In 1961, with the possibility of a championship title within the Packers' grasp for the first time since his arrival, my dad learned that three of his players—Paul Hornung, Boyd Dowler, and Ray Nitschke—were being called to military service and would miss the second half of the season. The news was disheartening, to say the least, and the remaining players were quietly resigning themselves to failure. My dad would have none of it, however, simply stating to the team that they were going to win. It was that simple: With or without their star players, they were going to pursue the title with everything they had, and they would win. And win they did, taking the title home to Green Bay for the first time since 1944.

To the winner there is 100 percent elation, 100 percent fun, 100 percent laughter, and the only thing left to the loser is resolution and determination.

No man, no matter how great he may be, can long continue to be successful unless he wins the battles, because the battles decide all.

I used to run the Green Bay Packers. At first, we didn't win. Later on, we won our fair share. Still, never as many as I wanted. *Which was all of them.*

Being part of a football team is no different than being a part of any other organization— an army, a political party. The objective is to win, to beat the other guy. You think that is hard or cruel—I don't think it is. I do think it is a reality of life that men are competitive, and the more competitive the business, the more competitive the men. They know the rules, and they know the objective when they get in the game. And the objective is to win— fairly, squarely, decently, by the rules, but to win.

My dad's philosophy of winning worked as well in a corporate boardroom as it did on the sidelines at Lambeau Field. He often was asked to speak to leaders of industry, to great acclaim. He looked at it as simply another way of teaching and loved the chance to share his thoughts with people from other walks of life.

WORK

Gary Knafelc on Lombardi: Lombardi works you so hard that when he tells you to go to hell, you look forward to the trip.

The harder you work, the harder it is to lose.

Desire has to be an inborn quality, but there are different methods to kindle it and keep it burning. Development of pride is one way. Hard work is another.

Our theory on how to develop a winning team is simple—work. We want to win, we play to win. . . . We are going to encourage, demand, insist that you give 100 percent effort in trying to win. You must be dedicated. Dedicated in the extent you are willing to work, sacrifice, cooperate, and do what you possibly can. . . .

Hard work was the first guarantee of success in my dad's book. The last three quotes—actually an excerpt from a sales-training film—give you some sense of what his players were greeted with from the first day of training camp to the last day of the season. Anybody who didn't work harder than he thought possible could expect to be shipped out of town on the next plane, train, or bus.

Work and sacrifice, perseverance, competitive drive, selflessness, and respect for authority are the price that each one must pay to achieve any goal that is worthwhile.

Success is the result of dedication to an ideal of working hard to correct weaknesses—working hard to understand what is required for success and working hard to achieve the goal of being perfect.

I'm going to ask you to work harder than you've ever worked before in your life, because the history of the National Football League *proves* that most games are won in the last two minutes of the first or second half. I'm going to expect a 100 percent effort at all times. Anything less than that is not good enough.

There is no substitute for work.

*Coach Lombardi thinking ahead to
the next series of offensive plays.*

YANKEES

We're going to be the Yankees of football!

This comment should come as no surprise from a man born and raised in New York City!

YOUTH

It has always been the function of youth to defend liberty and innovation, and the function of the old to defend order and tradition, and the function of the middle-aged to stay status quo.

More than three decades after my father made this statement, it still rings true. The youth of America are once again defending our liberty in Afghanistan and other places where terrorism lurks. And it's good that some old folks remind us of the traditions that make this country great. I'd like to think that some of the ideas contained in this book do that.

But there's a warning here, too. Adhering to the status quo and resisting change—not cosmetic change or change for the sake of change but the real change and growth that will keep this country great—also need to be guarded against in our fight for freedom and security in this country and around the world.

PAGE 18

You gotta remember one thing: If you're going to exercise authority, you've got to respect it. Wiebusch, John (editor). *Lombardi*. A National Football League Book, distributed in 1971 by Follett Publishing Co., Chicago. p. 122.

PAGE 21

I don't want any bad apples in my organization. I get one [bad] apple in the bushel over here, and the rest of them will start rotting, too. Wiebusch, John (editor). *Lombardi*. A National Football League Book, distributed in 1971 by Follett Publishing Co., Chicago. p. 48.

PAGE 22

Your consistent unwillingness to settle for anything less than excellence will always serve as an inspirational beacon for all of us who played for you. From an undated letter from Bart Starr to Vince Lombardi.

PAGE 34

He was the greatest psychologist. Maraniss, David. *When Pride Still Mattered*. Simon & Schuster, Inc. New York: 1999. p. 378.

PAGE 52

He refuses to accept defeat, even when he is defeated. I think he really believes that if the game goes on for another five minutes, he can win. It makes a difference to play under a guy like that, I can tell you. Dowling, Tom. *Coach: A Season with Lombardi*. W.W. Norton & Company, Inc. New York: 1970. p. 288.

PAGE 59

Of all the lessons I learned from Lombardi, from all his sermons on commitment and integrity and the work ethic, that one hit

home the hardest. I've found in business that only 15 or 20 percent of the people do things right all the time. The other 80 or 85 percent are taking short cuts, looking for the easy way, either stealing from others or cheating themselves. I've got an edge, because whenever I'm tempted to screw off, to cut corners, I hear that raspy voice saying, "This is the right way to do it. Which way are you going to do it, mister?" O'Brien, Michael. *Vince.* William Morrow and Company, Inc. New York: 1987. p. 383.

PAGE 64

I'll never give a game to an AFL team, and if you can't get emotional about what you believe in your heart, then you're in the wrong business. Wiebusch, John (editor). *Lombardi.* A National Football League Book, distributed in 1971 by Follett Publishing Co., Chicago. p. 94.

PAGE 108

There is no laughter in losing. Wiebusch, John (editor). *Lombardi.* A National Football League

Book, distributed in 1971 by Follett Publishing Co., Chicago. p. 56.

PAGE 116

The shoutings, encouragements, inspirational messages, and vindictive assault on mistakes transcended the walls of our dressing rooms, but in the privacy of those same rooms to have known the bigger man—kneeling in tearful prayer with his players, after both triumph and defeat—was a strengthening experience that only your squads can ever fully appreciate. From an undated letter from Starr to VL.

PAGE 117

It's the motivation that's the thing, and he knew just the right words, just the right approach to me. He knew how to handle me just like a parent handles his children to get the maximum out of them. Just the right approach to get me to listen, that was it. And he motivated me to the maximum. I don't think I could have given more. Wiebusch, John (editor). *Lombardi*. A National Football League Book, distributed in 1971 by Follett Publishing Co., Chicago. p. 171.

PAGE 149

The harder you work, the harder it is to surrender. O'Brien, Michael. *Vince*. William Morrow and Company, Inc. New York: 1987. p. 194.

PAGE 154

You might reduce Lombardi's coaching philosophy to a single sentence: In any game, you do the things you do best and you do them over and over and over. Wiebusch, John (editor). *Lombardi*. A National Football League Book, distributed in 1971 by Follett Publishing Co., Chicago. p. 49.

PAGE 172

He left no doubt what he expected, and—more important—explained why. Briggs, Jennifer. *Strive to Excel*. Rutledge Hill Press. Nashville: 1997. p. 110.

PAGE 172

Everything has a reason, a meaning. It makes it much easier to play the game. Dowling, Tom. *Coach: A Season with Lombardi.* W.W. Norton & Company, Inc. New York: 1970. p. 215.

PAGE 175

Lombardi explained that some of the players on the team were going to be famous, some obscure, but everyone was equally important. For us to succeed, we had to place our personal goals behind those of the team. We had to pick each other up and push each other to higher levels. Briggs, Jennifer. *Strive to Excel.* Rutledge Hill Press. Nashville: 1997. p. 54.

PAGE 193

Lombardi works you so hard that when he tells you to go to hell, you look forward to the trip. Lombardi, Vince. *Run To Daylight.* Simon & Schuster Inc. New York: 1963. p. 171.